Soviet Jewry
Today and Tomorrow

Soviet Jewry
Today and Tomorrow

BORIS SMOLAR

The Macmillan Company, New York, New York

Collier-Macmillan Limited, London

301.451
S666s

The Macmillan Company
866 Third Avenue, New York, N.Y. 10022
Collier-Macmillan Canada Ltd., Toronto, Ontario

Library of Congress Catalog Card Number: 70-151164
First Printing
Printed in the United States of America

Contents

2 3 0 / 1

Foreword

THIS IS THE STORY of three million Jews in the Soviet Union who are being considered by their government as "suspicious elements" and are being treated as such. It is an inside story written against the background of my years of work in Moscow as an American correspondent, and based particularly on my latest visit to the Soviet Union at the end of 1968.

In this book I attempt to present the picture of the life of Soviet Jews in the light of conversations with Soviet officials, writers, editors, scientists, students, workers, religious Jews, nonreligious Jews, and Jewish members of the Communist Party. I made a study of all problems affecting Jewish life in the U.S.S.R. In bringing out these problems, I attempt to give the official Soviet view on them, the views of various elements in Soviet Jewry, my own observations, and a look into the future.

From the chapters in this book the reader will learn that, at best, the Jews in the Soviet Union are a frightened people. He will see clearly why every Soviet Jew—be he an ordinary citizen or a scientist engaged in important work for the country—is kept under suspicion. He will realize what the real motive is behind the Soviet's marking the word "Jew" on identity documents of each Jewish citizen and what this means to the Jews. He will also get an idea as to whether this system will ever be abolished by the Soviet Government.

The reader will get a picture of the inequities practiced against Jews in various fields of Soviet life. He will be able to evaluate the mood of Jews in the Soviet Union, who are essentially loyal citizens but who nevertheless feel themselves—even when they hold higher positions—to be second-class citizens. He will also be able to judge what the future holds for the three million Soviet Jews—whether they will survive the discriminations practiced against many of them; whether they will disappear as Jews within a generation or so by assimilation forced upon them through the suppression of their culture; and whether they will emigrate in large numbers, if permitted to do so by the Soviet authorities.

Among the subjects touched upon in this book is also the ultimate aim of the Soviet Government with regard to Israel. Talks with Soviet officials in Moscow reveal a very different aim than the one generally accepted in the United States and at the United Nations. An evening spent with a young Arab who is being trained in Moscow—and a second evening spent with a group of his colleagues—reveals most interestingly his mentality and the purposes for which he and his colleagues are being trained in the Soviet Union.

The reader will also get an understanding why anti-Semitism is stronger in the Soviet Ukraine than in any other part of the Soviet Union. He will discover how secessionists in the Ukraine are using anti-Semitism as camouflage in their ambitions to have the Ukraine secede from the U.S.S.R. into an independent Ukrainian Republic, and to secure a position similar to that of Poland, Rumania, Hungary, Czechoslovakia, and other Soviet-dominated neighboring countries, which are nominally independent of Moscow.

The reader will become aware of the price that Moscow has paid to Ukrainian nationalists by quietly making, with no publicity whatsoever, the very important territory of the Crimea a part of the Ukraine. The Crimea is a most beautiful part of Russia. It is there where the Czar had his vacation residence and where the historic Roosevelt-Churchill-Stalin talks took place during World War II, concluding with the Yalta agreement. For generations, the Crimea has also been looked upon by Russia as a military bastion because of its ports and fortresses in cities like Sevastopol, Simferopol, and others.

Above all, the reader will learn one of the basic reasons why the Jews—all the Jews—in the Soviet Union are classified as a "suspicious element" in the Kremlin, not trustworthy in case of war with the United States. The possibility of a war between the Soviet Union and the United States is not excluded by Soviet leaders, and the belief among them is that the Jews in the Soviet Union will, in case of such a war, be on the side of the United States, because they have many relatives there.

The view that Soviet Jews are an element with strong ties to the United States in time of war originated with Stalin who became strongly anti-Jewish during the last years of his life. The same view was held by Nikita Khrushchev, Stalin's successor, who openly expressed it to Communist leaders from foreign countries who sought to intervene with him for equal treatment of Jews in the U.S.S.R. This is still the view held by the Soviet rulers of today.

This view has been strengthened since the establishment of the state of Israel in 1948, to which the Soviet Government was the first to give full diplomatic recognition. The Soviet Union broke off diplomatic relations with Israel twice since that time and is now openly and actively on the side of the Arabs, supplying them with modern arms and instructors to fight Israel. On the other hand, the Jews in the Soviet Union, although maintaining no contact with Israel now, are in their great majority sympathetic toward Israel.

Their friendly feelings toward the United States and their sympathy for Israel make them, in the eyes of the Soviet rulers, potential enemies of the Soviet Union. They are being looked upon in the Kremlin with the same suspicion as the Volga Germans were looked upon by Stalin shortly before the war between Soviet Russia and Nazi Germany, when Stalin ordered their deportation from the Volga region to remote parts of the U.S.S.R.

The Jews in the Soviet Union are not aware of the suspicion under which they are kept. However, they feel themselves as inferior citizens by the treatment they are given in being eliminated from high positions in the army, and in having all sensitive positions—in the foreign service and even in the party ranks—closed to them.

High Soviet officials do not admit that they are creating a "Jewish problem" in their country; they assert that there is no such thing as a "Jewish problem" existing in the Soviet Union. The chapters that follow show to what extent their assertion is wrong.

Soviet Jewry
Today and Tomorrow

Introduction: Visit and Revisit

I WAS BORN IN RUSSIA. During the First World War, I was a correspondent on the Russian-Austrian front. I witnessed the fall of the Czarist regime, the Kerensky Revolution, and the Bolshevik Revolution. Later I witnessed the occupation of the Ukraine by the German Army, the chaotic retreat of the German Army, the pogrom on Jews under the Petlura regime in the Ukraine. I saw the Polish troops march into the Ukraine and retreat a few months later to the gates of Warsaw driven by the Red cavalry under the command of the man with the fierce mustache, Soviet General Semyon Budenny.

When ten years later I came from New York to Moscow as an accredited correspondent of Pulitzer's *New York World* and of the Jewish Telegraphic Agency, the United States had still not recognized the Soviet Union. There were at that time no American Ambassador and no American consulates in the Soviet Union to protect American citizens. We were a small group of representatives of the American press, each of us working in Moscow at his own risk. The group included William Reswik, correspondent of the Associated Press; Eugene Lyons of the United Press; Edward Deuss of the International News Service; Louis Fisher, who wrote for *The Nation;* Walter Duranty of *The New York Times;* William Henry Chamberlin of *The Christian Science Monitor;* and myself.

Permission to travel around the country was given to me by the Commissariat for Foreign Affairs in Moscow, and at one time I carried out an assignment to visit thirty cities in the Soviet Ukraine and in Byelorussia. I also traveled from the Soviet-Polish frontier to the remote borders of China and outer Mongolia. And I crossed the Soviet Union all the way from the spot where the country meets in a triangle with the borders of Rumania and Poland to as far as the border of Afghanistan, in Middle Asia.

I was among the foreign correspondents who were permitted by the Soviet authorities, in 1930, to visit "the forbidden land of Bukhara"—a region which had remained untouched by European culture through the passage of thousands of years. This colorful region, known for its silks and carpets, was closed to foreigners even under the Czarist regime. The Soviet Government continued this tradition of secrecy with regard to Bukhara for economic, political, and strategic reasons. Only during World War II, when the Nazi armies invaded a large part of the European territory of the U.S.S.R., were some Russians evacuated to Bukhara as refugees.

I was also among the few foreign diplomats and journalists who were invited by the Soviet Government to cross the Turkestan Desert on the first trip of the Turksib train, linking Turkestan with Siberia. It was the most interesting trip I ever made. Our special train was escorted by soldiers who kept a twenty-four-hour guard on the water cisterns attached to the train, since drinking water was the most precious thing in the desert. During our trip we came across small groups of nomads scattered here and there under torn tents when not wandering in search of water.

I was in the Soviet Asiatic Republics of Uzbekistan, Kazakhstan, and Turkmenistan. I visited the distant city of Alma Ata and looked up the house where Leon Trotsky lived in exile under the Stalin regime prior to being permitted to leave the Soviet Union for Turkey, from where he made his way to

Mexico, only to be assassinated there by a Stalin agent. I also visited the colorful city of Tashkent and the "golden city" of Samarkand—built more than five thousand years ago— with its beautiful centuries-old towers in colorful mosaic. This city was taken by the Mongol ruler Genghis Khan in 1221. You can climb there to the grave of Tamerlane, the lame Asiatic ruler who made the city his residence and whose hordes invaded Europe in the fourteenth century as far as Turkey and the Volga, conquered Syria, and reached India. Samarkand has been under Russian rule since 1868, but not open to foreigners until World War II.

In 1931 I obtained a statement from Stalin on his views with regard to anti-Semitism. At that time Stalin was not as para-noic as he was during the last years of his life, when he dis-played definite anti-Jewish feelings. In his statement, written on January 12, he spoke strongly against anti-Semitism as "a phenomenon profoundly hostile to the Soviet regime." On January 14, 1931, the statement was published in *The New York Times* and in other leading newspapers all over the world. However, it was not carried by the Soviet press. Vya-cheslav M. Molotov, who later became Stalin's Foreign Minis-ter, quoted it—for the first time—about six years later in addressing a session of the Soviet Congress in the Kremlin in November 1936. It then appeared in *Pravda* on November 30, 1936.

I was often received by the late elderly Soviet President Mikhail Kalinin and even more often by Vice-President Peter Smidovitch, one of the old-time intellectual Bolsheviks, a gen-tle, aging man who headed the government body that con-ducted the settlement of "declassed" Jews on land as farmers in the Crimea and in the Ukraine. As an American correspon-dent, I had entrance to the opening sessions in the Kremlin of the WZIK, the All-Soviet Central Executive Committee, at which Stalin and other top Soviet leaders reported to the delegates from all over the country on internal and foreign af-fairs. I also had access to the Red Square on the First of May and on the October commemoration days to observe the mil-itary and civilian mass celebrations at close range from the seats erected for foreign diplomats alongside the Lenin Mausoleum, where Lenin's body lies mummified for the view of millions of people who come from all parts of the Soviet Union and stand for hours in long lines to get in to see it.

I often had my skirmishes with the Soviet censorship and at one time they canceled my accreditation as correspondent of the *New York World* but not as correspondent of the Jewish Telegraphic Agency. They were angered over a report I sent on Stalin to the *New York World*, which featured it as the main Page One story on May 2, 1929. I was given to understand that Stalin personally was "strongly displeased" with this report. However, the *New York World* insisted that I be permitted to continue my work and after several weeks of pressure my accreditation was restored.

In 1930 I was instrumental in the dissolution of the Yevsekzia, the Jewish Section of the Communist Party in the U.S.S.R., which has been held responsible by Jews throughout the world for stimulating the conversion of synagogues into atheist clubs and for persecuting rabbis and former Jewish merchants. I was similarly instrumental in influencing Soviet Vice-President Smidovitch—who was also the Commissar for Religious Affairs—to issue instructions to exempt Jewish settlers in the colonies in the Crimea and in the Ukraine from compulsory work in the fields on the first Collectivization Day, which fell on October 14, 1929, coinciding with Yom Kippur, the holiest Jewish religious holiday. For this I was editorially attacked by the leading Jewish Communist newspaper in Moscow, *Emes*, which was closed down in 1938.

Revisiting the Soviet Union in October 1968, I had the opportunity to study the situation of the Jews there by speaking to many of them and to Soviet officials, and by visiting Jewish homes and a number of Soviet institutions. I talked with at least two hundred Jews. They were of various professions and of various ages. There were among them university students, writers, holders of government positions, office workers, factory workers, cultural workers—men and women. There were some religious Jews and even Jews who insisted on conversing with me in Hebrew.

I succeeded in discussing the Soviet stand on Israel with high officials—in the Soviet Union today "Israel" is an "ugly word," which people try to avoid even in private conversations—and was given revealing information. Naturally, I discussed with Soviet spokesmen the question of anti-Semitism in the Soviet Union, discrimination against Jewish youth in universities, suppression of Jewish culture, inequality in the treatment of the Jewish religion, prevention of reunion of Jewish families through emigration, and other delicate subjects on which I found the Soviet regime to be very sensitive. I even had a chance to spend several hours with Arab students being trained in Moscow for military purposes and was invited by them to visit their dormitory. They spoke perfect Russian and very good English.

I was invited to private Jewish homes for dinner and I also had drinks with Soviet writers, some of whom presented me with their books inscribed "in friendship." I was among the twelve thousand Jews, mostly young students—boys and girls—who crowded the Moscow synagogue—and the entire block on which the synagogue is situated—on Simchas Torah evening, presenting an unforgettable scene of merriment within the synagogue and of dancing the Israeli "Hora" outside the synagogue until after midnight under a torrential autumn rain which did not, however, have any effect on their jolly mood.

Several factors helped me very much in my mission: knowledge of the Russian language, the fact that my name was known to numerous authors and editors in Leningrad and Moscow, and the fact that when speaking to Soviet authorities I emphasized that I had come primarily to study the status of the Jews in the U.S.S.R. and intended to write about it. In speaking Russian I did not try to pose as a Russian. I always made it a point to start the conversation by informing the people with whom I spoke that I was an American interested in taking a look at the situation of Soviet Jewry from the "inside."

Some Jews were hesitant to talk to me when they learned that I was a Russian-speaking American. Others, on the other hand, were very frank in talking with me. They welcomed the fact that they could converse with me in Russian, since most of them knew no English. This was especially true for the Jewish youngsters. They do not understand Yiddish either, so my talking to them in Russian bridged the gap between us.

Some of the elderly Jews whom I met were extremely cautious at the beginning of our talks. With them, my command of Russian worked the other way around. Obviously they did not trust me at the beginning because of my fluent Russian, although they were told that I was an American Jew. To them, any Soviet intelligence agent might pose as an American who speaks Russian.

At least two such Jews—one in Moscow and one in Kiev —tested me by asking in Hebrew whether I also spoke Hebrew. When my answer was "Yes," they began to speak to me in Hebrew. It was a poor Hebrew but very understandable. After conversing with one of them for a time in Hebrew, I suggested that it might be easier for him to talk to me in Yiddish. He rejected the suggestion.

"It is so seldom that I have a chance to converse in Hebrew," was his argument for using Hebrew as the language of our conversation. Hebrew has been banned in the Soviet Union since the first days of the Revolution.

Only upon my landing at the Leningrad airport—my first stop on Soviet soil—did I insist on speaking English. There was a reason for that. If you are an American, the formalities are gotten over with much more easily if you speak English.

◆ ◆ ◆ 2

Leningrad's Hebrew Secrets

AN AIR OF MYSTERY surrounds the state library building in Leningrad, named for the Russian author Saltykov-Shchedrin. No foreigner may enter its portals; even Soviet citizens are not admitted unless they have a pass. To secure such a pass one must be a scholar or a scientist, and even then he must have a letter from the institution where he works asserting that his research is important to the interests of the state.

The secret behind this most famous library—it ranks third in importance after the British Museum in London and the Bibliothèque Nationale in Paris—is that it contains documents and books which the Soviet Government does not want anyone to see, except by special permission. These include ancient and extremely valuable Hebrew books and manuscripts. Among them is the world's best collection of the "Geniza," the centuries-old sacred and secular Hebrew material found in Cairo in the nineteenth century in the ruins of an old building which was originally a church and was transformed in 616 c.e. into a synagogue.

Before the recent discovery of the now famous Dead Sea Scrolls, the Geniza was considered the most important collection of ancient Jewish documents, letters, and literary remains.

7

There is hardly a branch of Jewish learning that has not been enriched by the discovery of the Geniza treasures, now dispersed among many libraries—including the British Museum, the French Academy, the Hungarian Academy of Science in Budapest, and the Jewish Theological Seminary in New York. The collection of Geniza fragments in the Leningrad State Library occupies an eminent position in the scholarly world.

I decided to seek entrance into this sanctum sanctorum of Soviet scholarship, although I knew that except for a few privileged scholars, among them Professor Abraham Katsh of the United States, the Geniza material has been inaccessible to foreigners. I knew that Soviet students studying Hebrew for various state agencies were doing a considerable amount of Hebrew research in the library. I wanted to see who in the Soviet Union was interested in making a career of studying Hebrew.

It was not easy to contact the proper authority. The director of the Hebrew section of the library turned out to be a woman. She spoke to me in Russian, since I told her that I was an American who could speak Russian. We spoke over the telephone. She asked me a number of questions. First, she wanted to know why I was interested in examining the Geniza Collection. I explained to her that I had examined such collections in London and in New York, and since I was now in Leningrad I wanted to see the Leningrad collection, reputed to be the best collection of all.

She wanted to know whether I was a scholar and, particularly, whether I knew Hebrew and Aramaic, the languages in which the material is written. I assured her that I knew Hebrew and Aramaic well enough to read the fragments. She then said that she would call me back in an hour. It was obvious that she had to inquire of higher authorities whether to admit me, as well as to check on me.

Within an hour I was notified to report to a certain room in the library and was told that a pass would be ready for me at the entrance to the building. It was. A policeman guarding the door warned me that the pass had to be stamped by the official who would receive me, otherwise I would not be permitted to leave the building.

The room was on the third floor. I found two people waiting for me; one was a woman and the other a young man. The woman—obviously the director with whom I had spoken earlier—started a conversation, repeating the questions I had been asked before over the telephone. She wanted to know what I knew about the Geniza, what collections I had examined in other countries, how the collection in the Leningrad library originated. (It was originally acquired by the Russian Archimandrite, Antonin Kapustin, who resided in Jerusalem when the Geniza material was discovered in Cairo.) There were other similar questions. When I had passed the "examination" successfully, she inquired: "You said that you wanted to see our collection because it is among the most important Geniza collections in the world. How do you know that ours is so important?"

I told her that New York University had just published a booklet devoted especially to the Leningrad collection and written by Dr. Katsh (now president of Dropsie University in Philadelphia). I had the booklet with me and read to her the very first paragraph, which said: "In the domain of the Geniza material, Russia occupies an eminent position not so much in quantity as in quality."

She was elated. "An American university should say this about us!" She beamed. She asked me for the booklet as a contribution to the library, and I gladly gave it to her.

The ice had been broken. I was asked no more formal questions. The doors would now be opened to me, I felt certain. Suddenly, something happened. The young man who had been sitting there silent turned to me and asked: "Are you an author? . . . Did you ever write any books?"

I told him that years ago I had written several books; they were children's books. I added that it was difficult to get them now because they were out of print.

"But we have them!" he exclaimed proudly.

"You have my books on your shelves?" I was astonished.

"Yes," he said. "Do you want to see them?"

He took from his desk a note on which numbers were jotted. They were numbers from the library catalogue under which my books were filed. I suddenly realized that while checking on me the library authorities had also checked on whether I had ever written any books and whether these books had been admitted to their library.

The young man called in one of the librarians, gave her the note with the numbers on it, and told her to bring the books. Within a few minutes all my books were brought in and put in front of me. I was amazed to see them. One of them was published many years ago, and I myself have no copy of it.

"You have more of my books than I have!" I said, taking the book into my hands. It looked as new as if it had just been printed. I explained to the man that I had no copy of it.

"We can microfilm it for you, providing you give us a book in exchange," he offered.

I wondered what book I could give in exchange to such a library, and I said so.

"Have any of your books ever appeared in Hebrew translation?" asked the young man.

I told him that two of them had seen Hebrew editions.

"Well," he beamed, as if he had discovered something of great value, "you mail us copies of the Hebrew editions, and we will mail you a microfilm of your book in exchange."

The fact that he could add something to the Hebrew Department of the library played no small role later, when I was shown around that section and saw the rare Hebrew books as well as Hebrew publications from Israel—all "forbidden fruit" to Soviet Jews.

Later on I also visited the Leningrad University, where Hebrew is taught in secret classes.

Fifty years after the banning of Hebrew in the Soviet Union, Leningrad University is still maintaining classes in Hebrew and students are graduating from there every year. Who are these students? Who are their teachers? What Soviet-born young man today is interested in studying Hebrew, the use of which is prohibited in the country?

Officials of the university are secretive on this subject. They do not let you visit the classes because they do not want you to see even the faces of the students. However, they assure you that "our professors are the best in the world of Hebrew knowledge." They vaguely admit that the students are trusted young men and women who have made up their minds to specialize in Middle Eastern languages in order to make a career of this subject in service to the state.

I asked for a list of the professors, but this is obviously considered as much a state secret as are the names and faces of the students. However, from sources in Moscow I later received a partial list. I was startled to find on it not only Jewish names, but also non-Jewish ones. None of these names were previously known to me as those of Hebrew scholars, with the exception of Professor Klavdia Starkova, a Russian woman who has a record in the scholarly world as being dedicated to the study of the history of the Jewish people. She has written much on Yehuda Halevi, the outstanding Hebrew poet of the early Middle Ages, and is now engaged in studying the Dead Sea Scrolls and translating some of them into Russian.

Another non-Jewish woman who teaches Hebrew at the Leningrad University is Greta Demidowa. Her specialty is Hebrew grammar. Gita Gluskina, another member of the faculty, also teaches grammar and directs the students in reading biblical texts containing folklore. She also lectures on the fundamentals of Hebrew poetry and on the medieval poetry of Yehuda Halevi, Moses Ibn Ezra, and Solomon Ibn Gabirol.

Professor Isaac Vinnikov, expert on Semitic languages, lectures at the university on biblical texts and introduced a course in spoken Hebrew into the curriculum. In addition to Hebrew he has also mastered Aramaic, Syrian, Phoenician, and Arabic. Assistant Professor Hillel Alexandrov teaches ancient Jewish history up to and including the period of the Spanish Inquisition. He also discovered archive materials concerning the famous Hebrew poets Yehuda Leib Gordon and Abraham Ber Gottlober, who died in Russia at the end of the last century.

There are a number of other faculty members specializing in Hebrew. They include Dr. Lev Pilsker, who is one of the supervisors of the graduation theses of the students of Hebrew language at the Leningrad University; Anatoly Gazov-Ginzberg, who is an assistant to Professor Starkova, and others, less known, some of whom are graduates of the university.

In a secluded reading room of the closely guarded Saltykov-Shchedrin Library I found some of the students of Hebrew at the Leningrad University. They were doing their research work at the library.

They were all young people, born in the U.S.S.R. many years after the Communist Revolution. I was not permitted to talk to any of them. (Nor are they permitted to talk among themselves when in the research room.) They were deeply immersed in reading scholarly Hebrew books, some of them in old Rashi typescript, which testified to the fact that the books are not of this century.

I asked one of the senior officials of the library what made these young Soviet students select the study of Hebrew culture for their future career in a country where Hebrew is taboo. His reply was that some of them do it because they are preparing to become archeologists, others want to be linguists, and still others expect to be assigned to government posts where the knowledge of Middle Eastern languages is important.

The Hebrew Section of the library also has a special section where magazines from the Middle East—including some published in Israel, in Hebrew and in English—are available. Among them I saw the Israeli Hebrew literary magazine, *Moznayim* and several Israeli periodicals dealing with medicine and archeology. There were no Israeli political publications. Nor did I see any Israeli newspapers displayed.

A catalogue of the library's Hebrew manuscripts, compiled by Yona Ginzburg, an expert in Hebrew, is now being prepared for publication. The first volume, edited by Professor Starkova, will include chapters dealing with Bible manuscripts and interpretations of the Scriptures. Other sections will cover works on rudiments of Hebrew grammar, lexicography, mathematics, and music. The second volume will be devoted to manuscripts on theology and philosophy.

Most of the library's Hebrew manuscripts are from the sixteenth century, but there are also some from earlier times. They reflect the cultural life of the Jewish people over a period of nearly nine hundred years. One can also find there items by Saadia Gaon, the celebrated Jewish scholar of the ninth century, fragments of the writings of Moses Maimonides, the great Jewish philosopher of the twelfth century, eleventh-century works on astronomy, and miscellaneous early writings on medicine and philosophy.

Jews in Leningrad

LENINGRAD, with its two hundred thousand Jews, stands outside the stream of Jewish life in the Soviet Union of which Moscow is the center. But the synagogue in Leningrad is larger and more beautiful than the Central Synagogue in Moscow. It is the largest synagogue in the entire U.S.S.R. and the most beautiful in all of Europe.

The Leningrad Synagogue was built under the Czarist regime, when the city was known as St. Petersburg. Only the richest Jews in the empire were permitted to settle there. Other Jews—except for a few with higher education, which was rare among Jews in those years—were banned from residence there. The wealthy Jews of the Russian capital, among them Baron Horace Guenzburg, banker and philanthropist, could afford to build a synagogue that had no equal in beauty in many countries.

The Leningrad Synagogue is today not what it was in the years of its glory, when the aristocracy of Russian Jewry played an important role in the Czarist capital in the fight for Jewish rights. (They were not to win that fight until the Czarist regime fell in 1917 and the Kerensky Government, which succeeded it, annulled the anti-Jewish restrictions.) A half century ago the symbol of Jewish wealth and of creative Judaism, the Leningrad Synagogue is today a symbol of Jewish decline.

The gates at the entrance to the synagogue are wrought iron and constitute a rare piece of art. They are decorated with heavily gilded Hebrew letters—and would occupy a prominent place in any museum. Now, however, they hang on broken, rusted hinges and are exposed to the possibility of being removed for scrap iron.

Inside the synagogue, you get the feeling that you are in a great temple of art. High, and richly decorated with religious inscriptions in golden letters in Hebrew, stands the Holy Ark. The forty-five hundred seats for worshipers and the artfully carved balconies for women give you the impression that you are in a luxurious opera house. I stood inside the immaculately kept house of worship and felt lost there in the ashes of its glory.

The synagogue is closed all week long, except on Saturdays and holidays, despite the fact that all its seats are sold out for the entire year. Leningrad is large and its Jewish residents live in various sections of the city. Some of those who subscribe for synagogue seats work on Saturdays and cannot attend the services. Thus, even on Saturdays the number of worshipers is small. It is not so on the holidays. On Rosh Hashonah, Yom Kippur, Passover, Sukkos, and Simchas Torah, the synagogue is full. The services are conducted by a cantor, who also directs a small chorus of middle-aged Jews.

The cantor—he visited the United States in 1968 with Rabbi Yehuda Leib Levin, chief rabbi of the Moscow Central Synagogue—is not a professional cantor. By profession he is an engineer working in a large Leningrad industrial establishment. Highly respected by the management, he is relieved of work on Saturdays and on Jewish holidays so that he may perform his cantoral duties in the synagogue.

The synagogue has a "bridal room"—a special room where marriages are performed in accordance with the Jewish tradition. It cannot be said that the number of such marriages is large, considering the fact that a substantial proportion of the Jewish population in the city is composed of youngsters, many of them students, indifferent to religion and to the question of mixed marriages. However, this designation of a ceremonial room is indicative of the fact that Jewish traditions are not yet completely dead in Leningrad Jewish families.

Alongside the Leningrad Synagogue, in the courtyard, is a small synagogue. There you can find a "minyan"—a quorum of ten worshipers—every morning and every evening. The worshipers I found there presented a pathetic picture. They were old, shabbily dressed, people of a world of long ago. They spoke among themselves in Russian—a habit of the old and better years when every Jew in the city spoke Russian only. However, when it came to praying, each of them recited the prayers in Hebrew with traditional Jewish fervor.

The administrator of the Leningrad Synagogue—an aged Jew with a long, patriarchal, snow-white beard—was busy lighting "Yahrzeit" candles, one after the other, dedicated to the memory of dead Jews. He placed the candles in rows along a wall close to the entrance of the sanctuary. Every now and then a middle-aged Jew rushed in from the street:

"I want to place a candle in memory of my parents!" he addressed himself to the administrator.

The old Jew took down the name of the parent, attached a note to a candle, lit it, and placed it in the row. The visitor then dropped some money into a large, locked tin box marked with the word "Yahrzeit" and rushed out without further word. One could see he had not come here to pray, but only to honor the memory of his father or mother in the ancient tradition.

The income from the "Yahrzeit" candles, the administrator told me later, helps to maintain the synagogue. Other income comes from the Jewish cemetery.

"When a Jew dies and his relatives want to bury him in our cemetery, they must make a contribution to the synagogue," the old man said. "We also have income from the sale of synagogue seats; they are always oversubscribed. Then we have a special 'repair fund' for the synagogue. Many contribute to this who are not even members of the synagogue. As you could see at the gates, our synagogue is in need of repairs."

He outlined to me the problems of the Jewish religious community of Leningrad and was gloomy about the future. "We still have a large number of Jews in our community dedicated to Jewish traditional life, but the young people are not among them," he said with a sigh. At the same time he expressed optimism that a good part of the Jewish youth, though without Jewish education, would continue to maintain their Jewish identity in their own way.

"Take the boys and girls who come here by the thousands for Simchas Torah, to celebrate the holiday," he pointed out. "They constitute an encouragement to us, people of the old generation. They make us feel that Judaism will not disappear in our country, although intermarriage is widespread and religion is discouraged." He spoke with tenderness of the younger generation, to whom Judaism is totally alien but who nevertheless acknowledge Jewish identity.

Many Jews still come to the synagogue today to mourn members of their families who perished from starvation or were killed by shells and bombs during the terrible years of 1941–42, when Leningrad, besieged by the German armies, was under constant fire from the enemy. The roster of Jews who fell during the heroic resistance given day and night by the people of Leningrad in their determination not to surrender the city to the Germans is very impressive. It is estimated that more than fifty thousand Jews were among the approximately three hundred thousand men, women, and children who perished during the frightful ordeal.

The German military command made special attempts to inflame anti-Jewish feelings among the people of Leningrad by dropping inciting leaflets over the city. German loudspeakers blasted their propaganda from the battlefront, asserting that the Nazi Army merely wanted to "liberate" Leningrad from "Jewish Bolshevism." These German anti-Semitic efforts were counteracted, however, by mass meetings inside the beleaguered city at which speaker after speaker lauded the Jewish civilians and soldiers defending the city.

Nazi newspapers of that period—such as the *Voelkischer Beobachter*, the chief organ of the Nazi party in Germany—are full of reports from the Leningrad front portraying the death-defying Jewish fighters as refusing to surrender alive. The purpose of these reports was not to glorify the Jewish heroism but to justify the merciless treatment of Jews captured on the battlefield. Some of the Russian survivors of the Leningrad siege who knew no pity in fighting the Germans around Leningrad reported that their Jewish comrades in arms fought even more ferociously than they did.

Many young Jews—some of them in military officers' uniforms today—still relate how as school children they helped to build fortifications on the streets of the city or worked in Leningrad factories producing armaments for the defense of the isolated city, which was dependent entirely upon local production. Elderly Jews still tell tales of horror of those days when nobody in the city knew whether he would live to see the next day or, for that matter, the next hour.

The attachment of the Leningrad Jews to their city goes back more than a hundred years to when, under the Czars, only a small number of privileged Jews—mostly industrialists and other people of wealth—were permitted to reside in what was then the capital of Russia. The city was known as St. Petersburg at the time. These several thousand Jews—the richest among the five million Russian Jews (the rest of whom were segregated, in those days, in sections of the country which became known as the Jewish Pale of Settlement)—made their city the cradle of Russian-Jewish culture. They formed, in 1863, the Society for Dissemination of Education among Jews in Russia. Known as OPE, the organization laid the foundation for modern Jewish education by maintaining a net of 260 schools in about 160 towns in Russia in which Jewish children had no access to general education. They formed a Jewish Historic-Ethnographic Society which played an important role in collecting and preserving Jewish art and folklore. They established the ORT, an organization for vocational training of Jews which was later developed into the international Jewish body now maintaining a worldwide complex of about 700 vocational training schools in twenty-two countries of the free world.

It was also in St. Petersburg that Baron Maurice de Hirsch established the Jewish Colonization Association in the 1880's to help many thousands of Jews to emigrate from Czarist Russia, where they lived in poverty and under constant oppression, and to establish themselves on farms in Argentina and other countries.

Although composed of Russian-speaking Jews, the St. Petersburg community was the first in Russia to publish a daily newspaper in Yiddish, *Der Fraind*, and a Hebrew newspaper, *Hamelitz*. Both papers were issued primarily for the Jews who lived in the "Pale of Settlement" cities and towns where Yiddish was the spoken language and Hebrew the language of scholars. For the Jews who were "Russified" and read Russian only, there were two excellent weeklies in the Russian language—the non-Zionist *Voskhod* and the Zionist *Rassviet*—both of which had a nationwide circulation. It was also in St. Petersburg that Jewish leadership enabled the publication of a sixteen-volume Jewish Encyclopedia in the Russian language more than sixty years ago.

Jewish ties with Leningrad are thus at least four generations old. They were strengthened after the fall of the Czarist regime in 1917, when the residential restrictions for Jews were abolished. They are built on the patriotic affection which this city of beauty and culture arouses in every resident of Leningrad. They are also built on Russian-Jewish history, which left a mark on the entire Jewish population in the whole of Russia.

• • • 4

Anti-Semitism in the Soviet Union

ANTI-SEMITISM HAS HAD its ups and downs in Russia, reaching a high point under the last Czar, during whose reign Jews were killed in pogroms in Kishinev, Odessa, and other cities. After the fall of the Czarist regime in 1917, anti-Semitism was combated by the short-lived Kerensky Government, under which Jews attained complete emancipation. It was outlawed later under the Soviet regime and was publicly condemned by Lenin in no uncertain terms. It was compared with cannibalism by Stalin.

Things began to change, however, especially during the last years of Stalin's life, when he developed a paranoic hatred of Jews. In 1948 he ordered the mass arrests of practically all Jewish writers and other intellectuals, the killing of many of them, and the banishment of others to their death in camps in distant Siberia. He liquidated all the existing Jewish cultural institutions. He prepared a plan for the mass deportation of the Soviet Jews to remote places in the Arctic region. He instituted, in January 1953, the notorious "Doctors' Trial"—involving six prominent Jewish and three non-Jewish physicians—with the aim of showing that the Jewish doctors plotted to poison him. It was taken for granted that the accused would be sentenced to death and that the sentence would serve as signal for a most brutal campaign against the Jews throughout the U.S.S.R.

The trial did not take place only because Stalin died the day before it was scheduled to open. He had suffered a stroke earlier at a meeting in the Kremlin when some of the top leaders of the Soviet Government—including Marshal Voroshilov, the President of the U.S.S.R., and Vyacheslav Molotov, the Foreign Minister—dared to oppose openly and strongly his proposal to have the Soviet Jews transferred en masse to remote parts of Siberia. Immediately after his death the trial was canceled, the physicians released and rehabilitated. With Stalin's death also died his anti-Jewish deportation plan, which had been a nightmare to Soviet Jewry.

Nikita Khrushchev, who succeeded Stalin, did not revive the deportation scheme. He rehabilitated some of the Jewish writers who under Stalin had been exiled to Siberia or put to death. However, he propagated an atmosphere of crude anti-Semitism by his cynical remarks about the "too many Abramoviches" in the government apparatus. He also did not hesitate to tell a delegation of the Canadian Communist Party that he agreed with Stalin that the Jews in the Soviet Union were a "risk" in case of a Soviet war with the United States.

He admitted that the Jews had fought valiantly against the Nazi armies on the Soviet battlefronts, but said that the situation could be different in a war with the United States because many Jews in the Soviet Union have relatives in the United States. It was he who saw to it that Jews did not occupy any position of importance in national and municipal institutions in the Soviet Ukraine.

The present Soviet Government of Kosygin-Brezhnev continues to maintain a policy of anti-Jewish discrimination which makes Jews feel that they are considered second-class citizens.

Jews in the Soviet Union are still being eliminated from the diplomatic service, from posts in the foreign office, from Soviet offices engaged in trading with foreign countries, and from advancement in military ranks. They are barred from virtually all positions considered "sensitive" except in the field of nuclear physics, in which Jewish scientists are numerous and needed. That Jews are making great contributions in this field was admitted even by Khrushchev during a visit to the United States in 1959. He told the National Press Club in Washington that Jewish scientists were taking the uppermost part "in launching the Soviet rocket to the moon."

When I asked a Soviet spokesman in Moscow why Jews were not given any posts in the Ministry of Foreign Affairs and in the diplomatic service, he denied that this was the case. He pointed out that the chief of the department for Latin American countries in the ministry was a Jew named Lev Mendelevitch. When I requested more Jewish names he could not produce them.

The same official tried to impress upon me his claim that there was no discrimination against Jews with regard to leading positions in the armed forces. He rattled off the names of half a dozen Jewish generals, mostly engineers. When I argued that these names have been known for more than a quarter of a century and asked for names of younger Jews in the top ranks of the military personnel he smiled and said: "These younger people are now captains; give them time and they will become generals."

Several years after the war there were still more than fifty Jewish generals and admirals listed in the Soviet armed forces, and even a larger number of colonels. A number of them were "liquidated" by Stalin in his postwar purges. Others were pensioned off. Today there may be one or two Jewish generals in active service and a few in medical and engineering units. One now finds a Jewish engineer, Veniamin Dymshitz, occupying the post of Deputy Chairman of the Council of Ministers of the U.S.S.R. and a few other engineers serving in high positions in industry.

The policy of nonadmission of Jews to "sensitive" fields in Soviet life is being practiced not only by the government but also by the Central Committee of the Communist Party. The party maintains two institutions where the students are trained for leading positions—in the country and abroad. One is the Higher Party School and the other is the Academy of Social Science. Both are in Moscow. The students are tested for political reliability before being admitted. No Jewish Communist is being admitted to either of these institutions. Nor are Jewish students accepted into the Foreign Service Institute or the Trade and Commerce Academy.

Jewish Communist leaders in Moscow naturally deny the existence of discrimination against Jews on the part of the government. They also deny the existence of discrimination in the treatment of Jewish culture, Jewish religion, admission of Jewish students into universities—although they feel very uncomfortable when presented with irrefutable facts. They consider it a deliberate attempt to defame the reputation of the Soviet Government when one speaks of anti-Semitism in the Soviet Union or even of anti-Jewish discrimination.

On the other hand, they admit that there is a phenomenon in the U.S.S.R. which they label "kitchen anti-Semitism." One of the Jewish Communist leaders was specific in explaining to me what is meant by "kitchen anti-Semitism."

"As you know," he said, "we have a housing problem in our country. We are building dwellings at a great tempo, and you can see thousands of new apartment houses in Moscow. But the shortage in housing is still acute. Many families still live in old buildings where the kitchen is shared by all the tenants on the floor. Naturally, when several women cook in the same kitchen, annoyances develop. A non-Jewish woman can sometimes, in arguing with a Jewish woman in the kitchen, lose her temper and call the Jewish woman 'Zhidowka' [an extremely anti-Semitic insult to Jews]. On the other hand, the Jewish woman can hurl at her non-Jewish partner in the kitchen the word 'Katzapka,' which is no less insulting to a non-Jew than the word 'Zhid' to a Jew. This we call 'kitchen anti-Semitism.' "

He went on to add that Jewish women are more sensitive to the word "Zhidowka" than non-Jewish women are to the word "Katzapka." Hence, he said, they consider anyone who ever called them "Zhidowka" in a moment of irritation to be a Jew-hater and an unmitigated anti-Semite.

"But can you call this anti-Semitism?" he asked me.

I told him that I recalled a time when people using the insulting word "Zhid" against Jews in public were punished under the Soviet law forbidding anti-Semitism. "What happened to this law?" I wanted to know. "Obviously the word 'Zhid' was at that time considered an expression of strong anti-Semitic feeling. Why is there no punishment for it now?"

An ordinary Soviet Jew whom I met on a street in Kiev gave a simple answer when asked whether there is anti-Semitism in the Soviet Union, especially in the Ukraine, of which Kiev is the capital. "I don't know the difference between anti-Semitism and anti-Jewish discrimination," he said. "To me they are both the same. If by anti-Semitism you mean physical violence against Jews, then my answer is 'No.' There is no such anti-Semitism. But if you mean existence of anti-Jewish feelings, then my answer is 'Yes.' There is plenty of anti-Jewish sentiment in the country.

"Jews," he continued, "get jobs anywhere now, because there is a shortage of labor. I myself am of retirement age. But I was asked to remain on my job because I am needed. I am a simple bookkeeper in an industrial enterprise. I see the books, I see the wages, I see the promotions. In our enterprise a Jew is seldom promoted, even if he is very good at his work. He stands less chance of being promoted than a non-Jewish worker who is less qualified. And do you know why? Because our director does not like Jews. He needs them as workers but he does not like them. Would you call this anti-Semitism or discrimination? To me they are both the same."

The voice of this Jew is the voice of many Jews in the U.S.S.R. today. They make no distinction between anti-Semitism and discrimination. It may be considered by some to be mere discrimination when Jews are not advanced in their positions, or when they are not admitted at all to certain "sensitive" positions. To the average Jew in the country this is an expression of anti-Semitism. He wants to be considered a citizen equal with other citizens. But he feels that he is not being given full equality, although he does not fail to stress that he has nothing to complain about with respect to making a living.

· · · 5

Anti-Semitism and the Secession
Movement in the Ukraine

ANTI-SEMITISM IS today stronger in the Ukraine than in any other part of the Soviet Union. This is due to the fact that among the Ukrainians there are many extreme nationalistic elements. These extreme nationalists are daydreaming of separatism and independence from the Soviet Union.

Stimulating this feeling of irredentist nationalism are primarily a group of Ukrainian intellectuals born and educated in Eastern Galicia—the part of Poland which was absorbed by the Soviet Union and which became an integral part of Soviet Ukraine after the war. While still under the prewar Polish regime—which was strongly anti-Soviet—these Ukrainian elements, with their seat in Lvov, for years advocated the secession of Soviet Ukraine from the Soviet Union. They conducted propaganda insisting on the unification of all territories populated by Ukrainians—in Russia, Poland, and the Carpatho-Russian part of Czechoslovakia—into an independent sovereign Ukrainian state.

After World War II, when Eastern Galicia and Carpatho-Russia came into Moscow's possession, the Kremlin incorporated these territories into Soviet Ukraine, thus fulfilling the age-long dream of Ukrainian nationalists for a "larger Ukraine." The dream was fulfilled, but not to the satisfaction of the extreme nationalists. The latter wanted more. Their ambition was to see a Ukraine reunified, not as a part of the U.S.S.R. but as an independent country.

Unable, under the Soviet regime, to conduct any irredentist movement openly, as they did when they were under Poland, the Ukrainian extremists from Galicia—who were trapped at the end of the war when all countries surrounding Galicia found themselves under the rule of Communist governments —began to camouflage their ultranationalistic propaganda by developing intensified anti-Jewish propaganda. In this respect they followed the tactics of Nazi Propaganda Minister Josef Goebbels. It was the Goebbels propaganda machine which, during the years when the German Army occupied the Ukraine, concentrated on spreading violent anti-Jewish agitation in order to win stronger backing for Hitler among Ukrainians in the occupied parts of Soviet Ukraine.

The Nazi propaganda method was to implant in the population of Soviet Ukraine the idea that the German army of occupation did not enter the territory to keep it occupied for Germany but to "liberate" the people from Moscow's "Jewish Bolshevik regime" and to declare the Ukraine an independent state. This line of propaganda was, incidentally, also applied by the Germans during World War I, under Kaiser Wilhelm, when the German armies marched into the Ukraine and remained there for a comparatively short time, being forced to withdraw in November 1918.

During their occupation of the Ukraine in World War I the Germans actually set up an "independent" Ukrainian Government in Kiev, capital of the Ukraine, with Pavel Skoropadsky, a nationalist Ukrainian, as head. The Skoropadsky Government did not last long and was followed by another "independent" Ukrainian Government headed by Ataman Semyon Petlura, whose regime was notorious for its pogroms on Jews.

With the Ukrainian population 83 percent illiterate at that time, the "independent" government of the Ukraine created by the German Army had no choice but to depend to a very great extent on Ukrainian intellectuals from Galicia, which in those years was not under Poland but under Austria. Since the Austro-German armies were united in World War I, the Ukrainian intellectuals from Galicia—who were Austrian citizens—had no difficulty following the German occupational forces into the Ukraine. In fact, they were encouraged to do so, since their ambition to see the Ukraine an "independent and sovereign state" served well the interests of Germany.

As part of their active participation in the "Ukrainization" of the Ukraine during the short period of the German occupation, the Ukrainians from Galicia also played no small role in the pogroms on Jews under the Petlura regime. They were organized in special military units of the "Independent Ukraine" and were known as the "Blue Coat Units" or "Siechevik Units." Whenever these units appeared in a Jewish-populated town, a pogrom was inevitable. According to fairly reliable accounts, there were more than eight hundred pogroms on Jews during Petlura's regime in 1918–20. The number of Jews massacred in these pogroms is estimated by Soviet data to have reached 180,000. With the fall of the Petlura regime, the "Blue Coats" disbanded and most of them retreated to Poland, fearing to remain on Ukrainian soil which had passed into the hands of the Red Army. They continued their irredentist propaganda from Lvov, which became a part of Poland after World War I. After the fall of his regime, in 1920, Petlura fled to Paris as a political émigré. He was shot there in 1926 by Samuel Schwartzbard, a Jewish watchmaker, who was acquitted on the basis of Petlura's atrocities against the Jews in the Ukraine.

The absorption of Eastern Galicia and its capital, Lvov, into Soviet Ukraine after World War II gave the leaders of the Ukrainian separatist movement in Lvov a new and excellent chance to make themselves felt in Soviet Ukraine, where many among the natives are still under the spell of the intense anti-Jewish propaganda the Germans implanted during their occupation of the Ukraine.

Some Ukrainians collaborated with the Nazis during the occupation and were even entrusted with guarding the notorious camps in which Jews were gassed. Others were satisfied to see the Jewish population of their towns decimated as a result of the Nazis' rounding up all the Jewish inhabitants and mowing them down in ravines which thus became mass graves. Although these latter Ukrainians constituted perhaps only a small minority of their people, the field for anti-Semitic propaganda in Soviet Ukraine nevertheless remained fertile for the Ukrainian dissidents. However, they were compelled to go underground with their movement for an "independent" Ukraine and disguised it as anti-Jewish propaganda.

So impressive was the anti-Jewish propaganda of the secessionist elements that Nikita Khrushchev, who was chairman of the Ukrainian Council of Peoples' Commissars and secretary of the Central Committee of the Communist Party in the Ukraine in the postwar years—before he succeeded Stalin as ruler in the Kremlin—found it necessary to appease the extreme nationalist Ukrainians in their anti-Jewish tactics rather than combat their strategy. He quietly eliminated Jews from official positions in the Ukraine so that secessionist elements should have no grounds to assert, as they did, that Soviet Ukraine was "run by Jews." He saw to it that Jews were given as few jobs as possible in municipalities. He suppressed any specific mention of Jews as victims of Nazi barbarities in the Ukraine, his purpose being to prevent their figuring in the war history of the Ukraine as the element which suffered most from the Germans during their occupation of the country. He did not even permit the description of the largest massacre of Jews in the Ukraine—the Babi Yar mass execution in which tens of thousands of Jewish men, women, and children of Kiev were killed in cold blood by the Germans.

Despite Khrushchev's efforts to prevent any publicity on this barbaric mass slaughter of Jews and thus to avoid strengthening sympathy toward Jews among Ukrainians, this tragic "episode" was immortalized—against Khrushchev's will—by the Soviet poet Yevgeny Yevtushenko in his epic poem "Babi Yar," which has been acclaimed throughout the world. It was to a ravine in Babi Yar, a suburb of Kiev, that the Jews were led from Kiev in large groups and mowed down. Khrushchev, in his policy of appeasing the extreme Ukrainian nationalists, saw to it that apartment buildings came up on the site of the covered ravine and that woods were planted there in order to wipe out this "episode" of mass murder from the memory of the Ukrainian people. Today only a small primitive stone marks the grave, and even this stone does not tell that the victims were Jews.

There were one and a half million Jews in Soviet Ukraine at the outbreak of the war in 1939. At least eight hundred thousand of them were killed by the Nazis during the years of the German occupation. Khrushchev, in his keynote address at the first session of the Supreme Soviet of the Ukraine, held on March 1, 1944, after the liberation of the Ukraine from the Germans, did not even refer to the fate of the Jews of the Ukraine under the Nazi occupation. He obviously did not want to "irritate" the Ukrainian extremists by implying even indirectly that the Jews had been the greatest sufferers during the Nazi period.

The lenient attitude taken by the Kremlin—before and since Khrushchev's rule in Moscow—with regard to anti-Semitism in the Ukraine has encouraged the Ukrainian extremists to a point where in 1963 an anti-Semitic book reminiscent of the type of anti-Jewish books published in Germany under Hitler appeared in Soviet Ukraine. It was published under the imprint of the Ukrainian Academy of Science, the highest and most recognized body of intellectuals in the country.

The book, entitled "Judaism Without Embellishment," was written by Trofim Kitchko, a Ukrainian nationalist. It was "illustrated" with caricatures resembling the vulgar anti-Semitic caricatures carried by *Der Stuermer*, the most disreputable anti-Jewish newspaper, published in Nazi Germany by the notorious Julius Streicher, who was sentenced to death as a leading Nazi war criminal by the Allied Tribunal at the Nuremberg trial of the principal Nazi leaders.

The Kitchko book has provoked worldwide criticism, even

among Communists, because of its viciousness, and the Kremlin was very much embarrassed by it, especially since the Soviet Government maintains that it considers anti-Semitic propaganda a criminal act. The ideological committee of the Communist Party in the U.S.S.R. has officially disassociated itself from this book and condemned it. Government spokesmen have "explained" that the book appeared only in the Ukrainian language and was never sold in Moscow or in any part of the Soviet Union other than the Ukraine.

Despite the apologetics from Moscow and the sensitivity shown by the Kremlin, nothing has happened to Kitchko. He was not put on trial for spreading anti-Semitism, as expected. On the contrary, five years later—in 1968—another of his books against Jews appeared in the Ukraine. It was after the Arab-Israeli Six Day War and Kitchko did not miss the opportunity to pour poison into the minds of the people of the Ukraine in the guise of writing against Israel and the Jewish religion. In January 1968 the Supreme Soviet of the Ukraine awarded him the highly prized "Certificate of Honor."

Literaturnaya Gazeta, a leading Soviet newspaper, described Kitchko—in an article in its issue of February 10, 1963—as "a scoundrel." The article said that during the Nazi occupation of the Ukraine, Kitchko worked for a theater in the Ukrainian city of Vinnitza and collaborated with the invaders. Subsequently he wrote a fictitious report on his activities in the underground, was discredited and expelled with ignominy from the Communist Party.

The fact that his second anti-Semitic book was published in Kiev in 1968, five years after his first book "Judaism Without Embellishment" was condemned in Moscow by the ideological committee of the Communist Party, indicates that he is under powerful local patronage in the Ukraine. His second book, which appeared under the title "Judaism and Zionism," was published this time not by the Ukrainian Academy of Science, but by the "Society 'Znamya' of the Ukrainian Soviet Socialist Republic" in Kiev. The title page says that the book was "approved for printing" on August 30, 1968, and that it was printed in sixty thousand copies. The book opens with an announcement that the volume "is intended for a wide circle of readers," which in Soviet parlance means that it is to be used for propaganda purposes by the apparatus of the Communist Party in the Ukraine. Its price is only fourteen kopecks, which is equal to about fifteen American cents at the Soviet official rate of exchange. As in the case of "Judaism Without Embellishment" Kitchko's "Judaism and Zionism" appeared in the Ukrainian language only, not in Russian.

During my 1968 visit to the Soviet Union I raised the Kitchko issue in my talks with Soviet officials. What interested me most was establishing to what extent the extremists in the Ukraine were really victorious in gaining independence from Moscow in important ideological areas, as suggested by the fact that Kitchko is continuing his line of propaganda despite the Kremlin's official condemnation of his first anti-Jewish book.

"It seems that Kitchko enjoys quite a backing in the Ukraine despite the stand of the Kremlin," I remarked. "A formal decision of the Kremlin could not so easily be disregarded in Soviet Ukraine unless some 'separatist' elements there have strong roots," I pointed out. I also referred to the fact that Premier Kosygin in July 1965 and *Pravda* in September 1965 had assailed anti-Semitism.

The answer I received sidetracked the issue. It was the usual stock-in-trade reply that the Kitchko book had been withdrawn from sale even in the Ukraine after the Kremlin's disapproval of it.

"But how do you justify the fact that such an outstanding institution as the Ukrainian Academy of Science saw fit to be the publisher of such a rabidly anti-Semitic book?" I continued to ask. "Does this not indicate that certain 'academicians' in the Ukraine are anxious to show their 'independence' from Moscow by deciding for themselves on a line of guidance in publishing books on ideological problems?"

The question was most embarrassing, but the answer was: "The book was not published by the Academy proper. It only carried the imprint of the Academy's publishing house. Kitchko is not a member of the Academy."

"That makes it even worse," I argued. "Why should the publishing house of the Academy publish a book by one who is not even a member of the Academy and thereby make anti-Semitism look respectable? Did not Lenin warn against anti-Semitism as a phenomenon dangerous to the Soviet system?"

I expressed the view that there must be a deeper implication in the publication of Kitchko's book in the Ukrainian language. The book had been printed in Lvov, the city where Ukrainian intellectuals have for many years preached secession from Russia and the creation of a "Samostoina Ukraina"—a free and independent Ukraine. Anti-Semitism in the Ukraine seems to be only a cover for this illegal movement in the Soviet Union, I ventured to say.

"You will notice," I continued, "that the book carries a significant line at the top of its opening page. The line reads: 'This book is intended for wide readership.' This means that it was considered propaganda material. The question is, by whom was it considered that important? Who are the elements that were interested in securing mass readership for it? Certainly not the Kremlin, which publicly repudiated the book. If not the Kremlin, then there must be elements in the Ukraine that do not see eye to eye with the Kremlin."

I then drew attention to the fact that the book is the work not only of a single person called Kitchko. From the cover page in the Ukrainian language, which I can read, it can be seen that it was edited by an editor named B. C. Tchumachenko and that it also had two "art editors"—M. O. Savchenko and B. M. Tepliakov—who approved the vile anti-Jewish cartoons which are even more reprehensible than the text of the book that contains them. Not to speak of the fact that all the material passed official censorship before going to press.

"Does this not show that there are in the Ukraine intellectuals—some in the position of political censors—who differ with Moscow on the question of hampering anti-Semitic propaganda?" I wanted to know.

The answers I received were vague. There was the insistence that Moscow does not appease the chauvinistic elements in the Ukraine at the expense of the Jews. However, I left Moscow with the impression that the Kremlin seems to be more concerned with the fact that Soviet Ukraine is the second largest republic within the Soviet Union than with taking harsh measures against anti-Semitic intellectuals in the Ukraine who are conducting open and persistent hate propaganda against the Jews.

The territory of the Ukraine is larger than France; it is larger than England, Belgium, Holland, Switzerland, and Denmark taken together. It has a population of forty-five million people, three-quarters of them Ukrainians. It has always been known as "the bread basket of Russia," even under the Czars. It is not only rich in agriculture but has also developed under the Communist regime into a major industrial area with coal mines, metallurgical industries, and oil fields, and with important ports on the Black Sea.

This has played no small role in Khrushchev's policy of appeasing extreme nationalists in the Ukraine at the expense of tolerating open anti-Semitism. This appeasement policy is being maintained even today, after the fall of Khrushchev, and this explains why the Kitchkos and their like remain unpunished—and are even honored—despite their vulgar anti-Semitism.

The Penal Codes of the Soviet Union provide for imprisonment for from six months to three years, or exile for from two to five years, for any attempt to sow anti-Semitism. This law was not applied to Kitchko, nor to any of the editors of his book, to the "artists" responsible for the ugly Nazi-like anti-Semitic caricatures in his book, nor the publishing house which published the notorious book. The toleration shown by Moscow to the Kitchko clique provides food for thought, since it constitutes a gap between what the Kremlin says against anti-Semitism and what it does.

The Jewish Religion in the Soviet Union

IN MOSCOW'S "GUM"—the huge state-operated department store facing the Kremlin on Red Square—you find reproductions in brass of famous Russian Orthodox churches. They are plaques produced as souvenirs by the Moscow state factory Znamya Revolutzii (The Banner of the Revolution) and are being sold at the equivalent of $1.85 each.

Don't look anywhere in the Soviet Union for plaques showing the imposing facade of the Moscow Synagogue or the beautiful aspect of the Leningrad Synagogue. Their reproduction would be considered by the authorities to be Jewish religious propaganda; hence it is out of the question for anyone, particularly a state factory, to make them.

In Zagorsk, the center of the Russian Orthodox Church, there is a factory producing ikons. They are being sold all over the country to religious Russians, the number of whom is still substantial among the older and middle-aged generations. They yield quite a profit to the church. Don't look for Jewish religious mementos anywhere—not for a Chanukah lamp, nor a mezuzah, nor anything with a Mogen Dovid (Star of David) on it. Their production is forbidden.

The Russian Orthodox Church maintains a factory for candles which are usually bought by religious Russians for placing before ikons in churches and at home. This, too, is a source of substantial income for the church. But can synagogues produce Yahrzeit candles which members of Jewish families place in memory of their dead? No, synagogues must buy the candles; they are not allowed to manufacture them.

The Russian Orthodox Church maintains its own printing plant and is permitted to print sermons, prayer books, and liturgical literature and to distribute these from its central headquarters in Zagorsk to churches all over the Soviet Union. The plant also prints religious calendars and even a monthly church publication. The leaders of the Jewish religion can hardly dream of such full privileges, though a Jewish prayer book was printed ten years ago in an edition of three thousand copies and was recently reprinted in ten thousand copies.

One does not necessarily have to be an Orthodox Jew to learn in Moscow the extent to which the Jewish religion is being muzzled as compared to the other religions in the Soviet Union. There is no question about the fact that Jewish religious activities in the U.S.S.R. are much more restricted than those of other religious groups, including the Old Believers, an old, Russian sect.

Officials of the Council on Religious Affairs—a government organ attached to the Soviet Cabinet—are very embarrassed when presented with the facts of discrimination. They claim that the position of the Jewish religion differs in no way from that of any other religion in the country. However, it is hard for them to deny that the spiritual head of the Russian Orthodox Church is permitted to go abroad often—to capital cities like Jerusalem, Istambul, Athens—in order to maintain personal contact with other Orthodox churches.

Nor can the officials of this Council, under whose supervision all religions in the U.S.S.R. are placed, deny that leaders of the Moslem religion are permitted often to visit Moslem countries abroad, and even to organize pilgrimages from the Soviet Union to Mecca. They must admit that the head of the Catholic Church in the U.S.S.R. met with no difficulties when he wanted to proceed to Vatican City to attend the Ecumenical Council.

At the same time no rabbi has ever been permitted by the Soviet authorities to visit Jerusalem or to participate in any Jewish religious conference abroad—even when other Communist countries permitted their rabbis to attend these conferences. Moscow's Rabbi Yehuda Leib Levin was, for the first time, permitted in 1968 to visit the Jews in the United States, but neither he nor his predecessor was ever permitted to proceed to Jerusalem. Inside the Soviet Union no conference of Jewish religious leaders has taken place during the past forty years.

I was especially interested to find out why the Soviet Government does not permit existing synagogues to govern themselves by means of a central Jewish religious body although other religions have been given such permission. In my view, Jewish religious life will cease to exist in the U.S.S.R. within twenty years if it is not directed by a central Jewish religious authority.

I posed the question of permitting the existing synagogues to establish themselves into a federation. I was presented with an answer reading: "The state does not prevent the formation of a central Jewish religious authority. It is a matter entirely for the worshipers to decide. They arrange their affairs and orders as they see fit."

This answer implied that if Jewish religious congregations actually wanted to establish a central body of their own, they could do it. It thus puts the blame for the lack of such an institution on the Jewish religious leaders in the Soviet Union. I doubt, however, that this statement contains the real explanation for having the synagogues isolated one from the other. Jewish religious leaders in the U.S.S.R. are naturally not in a position to challenge this allegation. For this reason, I did not even attempt to ask Rabbi Levin whether he would confirm or deny it. However, I learned that as far back as 1960 Jewish religious leaders started conversations with the authorities on the question of creating a central religious body. So far, nothing has come out of these talks.

Rabbi Levin is a man over seventy-five years of age and should be spared embarrassment. The only way to bring clarity into the pertinent question of whether the synagogues in the Soviet Union can establish their own central religious body—as Soviet officialdom in Moscow claims—is to have important Jewish organizations in the United States submit this question in writing to the Soviet Ambassador in Washington. An answer from him, which will naturally be based on official information from his government, will once and forever clarify the issue.

The matter is of utmost importance to Jewish religious existence in the U.S.S.R. Without a central religious body, Jewish religious life in the Soviet Union will definitely melt away and disappear in a short time. Remnants of it will be found only in Bukhara and in the Caucasus, where the synagogues are ancient and Jewish tradition more rooted than in any other part of the country.

Soviet officials with whom I discussed the status of the Jewish religion in the Soviet Union tried to assure me that the state does not interfere at all in religious affairs. Soviet citizens, they claimed, are free to worship as they see fit or to be atheists. "This is recorded quite categorically in the Constitution of the U.S.S.R.," one of them pointed out.

The same official asserted that the Jewish religion is not being attacked in the Soviet Union and that antireligious literature in general pursues solely the aim of "enlightenment," without any attempt to hurt the feelings of religious people. This is not exactly the case. Soviet newspapers in the Ukraine and in Byelorussia quite often permit themselves to carry articles on Jewish religion which are offensive to Jews. Not to speak of the notorious book, by the Ukrainian writer Trofim Kitchko, "Judaism Without Embellishment."

To support the assertion that the Jewish religion receives treatment equal with that given other religions in the U.S.S.R., the official rattled off to me a long list of cities in the Soviet Union where synagogues function unmolested. The list includes distant cities in Siberia, in the Urals, in Tashkent and Samarkand, in Bukhara, and in Soviet Georgia, as well as in the European part of the country. Cities like Moscow, Leningrad, Kiev, Odessa, Riga, Minsk, and Vilna were, of course, also listed.

"Moscow," he pointed out, "was known in Czarist times as the city of 'forty times forty' Russian Orthodox churches. Today there are only about forty churches functioning in Moscow as compared with the large Jewish choral synagogue and two smaller Jewish houses of worship in the city. Compare the proportion of the Jewish population in Moscow to the general population and you will see that the Jews have no basis to complain. Many churches have been closed down in Moscow since the days of the Revolution, but no synagogue."

"But what about the fact that in 1956 a report at the United Nations said that some 450 synagogues existed throughout the Soviet Union, while today their number is only about sixty?" I asked.

"This is not so," the official replied. "There have not been 450 synagogues in the Soviet Union since the year the Nazi armies occupied the Ukraine, Byelorussia, Crimea, and other parts of our country. The German occupation forces destroyed the entire Jewish life in those cities, including the Jewish houses of worship. They killed all the Jews except those we managed to evacuate from the cities into the interior before the Germans entered there. When we liberated these cities later, we found no Jews there and, of course, no synagogues."

In his estimation there are today about a hundred synagogues still functioning in the U.S.S.R. He emphasized that neither the central nor the local Soviet authorities hamper their religious activities.

"You can see for yourself that we even permit huge religious street celebrations in front of the synagogues on the Jewish holiday of Simchas Torah," he cited as example.

"This is all true about the religious street demonstrations on Simchas Torah, but they are permitted only in Leningrad and in Moscow. Why not in Kiev? Why not in Odessa? Why not in other cities?" I wanted to know.

I received no satisfactory answer to this question. The Jews in those cities, the official said, are perhaps not as keen on celebrating the holiday as the many thousands of Jews who participate in the Simchas Torah celebrations in Moscow and Leningrad. I was told later in Kiev, a city with a Jewish population of two hundred thousand, that this is not the case. The Kiev authorities simply do not permit any religious celebrations in the street.

In 1969 the Soviet Government began to display more attention to some—but not to all—Jewish religious needs. After many years of making it difficult for Jews to bake matzo, the traditional unleavened bread, for Passover, and after prohibiting altogether the baking of matzo in 1962—an act which provoked Jewish protests all over the world—the authorities did not in any way whatsoever hinder Jews from securing matzo during Passover 1969. It was the first time in many years that religious Jews in the Soviet Union had no reason to complain that the government was preventing them from observing Passover in a traditional manner.

Also for the first time, the central Soviet authorities recently indicated that they may permit the sending of a young Jew to Hungary to study for the rabbinate at a Jewish theological seminary there, after which he would return to Moscow as an ordained rabbi. More than 90 percent of the synagogues in the Soviet Union have no rabbis today because there is no Jewish seminary for training rabbis. The very few rabbis who are still alive are—like Rabbi Levin in Moscow—men over seventy-five. Several years ago an effort was made to establish at the Moscow Synagogue a seminary for training younger men for the rabbinate, but the effort evaporated when Moscow local authorities made it difficult for the less than a dozen theological students to secure residential permits—and the students were primarily from the distant places of Bukhara and Georgia. In Hungary, under the present Communist regime, there still functions a Jewish theological seminary which has been in existence for generations. The Moscow Government risks nothing by permitting one young religious Jew to proceed to this neighboring Communist country to study for the rabbinate.

Similar to the present status of the synagogue in the Soviet Union was the situation of the Armenian Church. For several years after the assassination of the Patriarch—generally called Catholicos—in 1938, the Armenians in the Soviet Union, whose number is approximately the same as the number of Jews there, had no Patriarch. In 1955 the Soviet authorities permitted the "importation" of a Patriarch from Rumania. Today the Supreme Patriarch of All the Armenians is Catholicos Vazgen I, who came to Soviet Armenia from Bucharest, where he was Archbishop. He was forty-five years old when he was brought from Rumania in 1955 to the Cathedral of Echmiadzin in Soviet Armenia, the seat of the Patriarch.

Although the Armenian Church now has a theological seminary in Echmiadzin with thirty-two students and a monastery with fifty-five clerics the Armenians claim there is still a shortage of priests, and the Patriarch has secured from the Soviet authorities "approval in principle" to invite an Armenian archimandrite from the United States for a period of service in Armenia. Whether such consideration would be given should a rabbi be needed to succeed the aged Rabbi Levin is rather questionable. A situation may therefore develop where the Jewish religious community in the Soviet Union will remain without a rabbi, as was recently the case in Sweden. The small Stockholm Jewish community had to bring a rabbi from the United States to serve its religious interests, since no rabbi was available in Sweden, where there are only about twelve thousand Jews, not all of them religious.

Incidentally, Rabbi Levin, who is considered the Chief Rabbi in the Soviet Union, makes it a point to emphasize that he is not the Chief Rabbi of Soviet Jewry but only the rabbi of the Moscow Synagogue. When he speaks he makes it clear that he does not represent all the Jewish religious communities. There has been no Chief Rabbi in the Soviet Union for many years because—unlike all other clergy in the U.S.S.R.— Jewish religious leaders cannot hold a nationwide conference to name a Chief Rabbi.

The first national gathering of Jewish religious leaders in the

Soviet Union was held in March 1971, more than fifty-three years after the Bolshevik Revolution. Some sixty heads of Jewish congregations from all parts of the Soviet Union were summoned to Moscow and met for six hours in the choral synagogue there to denounce Zionism and the State of Israel. The gathering was obviously arranged by the Soviet authorities for the specific purpose of counteracting Jewish protests abroad against anti-Jewish discriminations in the Soviet Union and the demand for free Jewish emigration from the U.S.S.R. to Israel, voiced a month earlier at the World Conference of Jewish Communities on Soviet Jewry, which took place in Brussels. No problems of Jewish life inside the Soviet Union were raised at the gathering in the Moscow synagogue and no naming of a Chief Rabbi was on the agenda of this first conclave of Jewish congregations.

Even if the Soviet Government would permit the sending of a young religious Jew to Hungary to be trained there for the rabbinate, this will by far not solve the acute shortage of rabbis in the country. When it comes to the question of training of rabbis the Jewish religion faces more limitations than any other religion in the Soviet Union, since all the other religious groups have no difficulty in maintaining theological seminaries.

The Jewish religion is also at a disadvantage since it is not permitted to have a printing shop, like other religions do, to produce liturgical and theological texts. Even the Armenian Church operates such a shop. The Protestant Church, which is also a minority church in the U.S.S.R., is permitted to get religious textbooks from Protestant groups in England and West Germany. No similar privilege is extended to the synagogues. The Moslems, who have two theological seminaries—one in Tashkent and one in Bukhara—print the Koran in a printing shop of their own. The publishing facilities maintained by the Russian Orthodox Church are extensive, as already noted.

While the synagogues cannot maintain any contact with Jewish religious groups abroad, the Russian Orthodox Church is not only permitted to do so but is even encouraged by the Soviet Government to maintain a Foreign Affairs Department of its own. The Kremlin is especially interested that contact should not weaken between this largest and official church—

which has twenty thousand parishes throughout the Soviet Union in seventy-three dioceses governed by seven Metropolitans, thirty-seven Archbishops, and twenty-nine Bishops—and Orthodox Churches in other countries. At present the jurisdiction of the Orthodox Church in the Soviet Union includes parishes in Israel, Turkey, Lebanon, Bulgaria, Yugoslavia, Austria, Hungary, and several other countries of Western Europe. It also has jurisdiction over a number of parishes in the United States and China, and it maintains missions in Japan and Korea. At the same time it also maintains contact with the World Council of Churches and its various branches in a number of countries, with the Anglican Church, and with the American Bible Society.

The Catholic Church in the Soviet Union—a minority church which has 1,235 parishes, most of them in Lithuania—maintains contact with the Vatican. The Moslem Church, with its eight thousand mosques in Central Asia, is not only encouraged to maintain contact with Moslem religious groups abroad but sends pilgrimages to Mecca on airplanes chartered by the Soviet Government. The Protestant Archbishop has been permitted to visit the United States, England, Sweden, West Berlin, and other Protestant communities abroad. The Baptist Church is permitted to maintain contact with groups in the United States, West Germany, and Scandinavia. It even sent a delegate to a Baptist conference in Brazil. The head of the Armenian Church is permitted to go to the United States and to visit cities like New York, Boston, Detroit, Chicago, Los Angeles, and San Francisco, where there are Armenian churches.

The Jewish religious community in the Soviet Union is of no importance to the Kremlin since it cannot exercise any influence on Jews abroad. Thus, while the government displays a comparatively benevolent attitude toward all other religions in the country, the Jewish religion is merely tolerated by the authorities as long as it exists, with the assumption that its existence will not be long since the young generation of Jews is far from being religious.

... 7

Jewish Culture in the
Soviet Union

AMERICAN JEWISH TOURISTS, when they come to Moscow, make it their business to visit the Central Synagogue, the only Jewish institution known to them. There is, however, another Jewish institution in the Soviet capital, a cultural institution. In fact, the only Jewish cultural institution existing in the Soviet Union. This is the Yiddish-language monthly magazine, *Sovietish Heimland*, a literary publication officially issued as the "Organ of the Association of Soviet Writers."

The Association is not a Jewish body, but it has Jewish writers among its members. It was chosen by the Soviet Government to be publisher of *Sovietish Heimland* because there is no Jewish group to whom the government could have entrusted this task. The publication of this only printed word in Yiddish was permitted in 1960, about twelve years after the liquidation by the Stalin regime of the entire organized Jewish cultural life in the country, when all Jewish cultural institutions were closed down and more than 220 Jewish writers and intellectuals were executed or sent to their death in Siberia. In the interval, no Jewish cultural life existed in the Soviet Union.

I sat in the office of Aron Vergelis, editor of *Sovietish*

Heimland and trusted Jewish Communist, and discussed with him the status of Jewish culture in the U.S.S.R. today. His magazine is at this time the only Jewish publication in the Soviet Union, with the exception of a small four-page newspaper, *Biro-Bidjaner Shtern*, appearing once a week in the remote Siberian region of Birobidjan. Why such limitations? Why has Jewish cultural life still not been fully restored to what it had been prior to the days of its brutal liquidation by Stalin? Why no public lectures in Yiddish? Why no public courses in Yiddish for those who might want them? Why are there no Yiddish textbooks? Why have the Yiddish state theaters, which were liquidated by Stalin, still not been reopened, so many years after Stalin's death? Why is the culture of the Jews not given the same treatment which all other national minority cultures enjoy?

Mr. Vergelis tried to explain to me that interest in Yiddish culture among Soviet Jews today is not at all comparable to what it was in the early years of the Communist regime, when there were hundreds of Yiddish state schools, three daily Yiddish newspapers, several Yiddish state theaters. He attributed the decrease in interest partly to the fact that for several years after the liquidation by Stalin of Jewish cultural life there was a vacuum during which Yiddish was replaced by the Russian language, even among Yiddish-speaking Jews. He also claimed that Jewish youth wants to have its education in the language of the country and is completely ignorant of Yiddish culture.

He told me that his magazine is printed in twenty-five thousand copies and proudly cited the names of a number of high Soviet Jewish officials who subscribe to it. These, however, are all people past the age of fifty. I reminded him that official Soviet data published in 1961 showed that 472,000 Soviet Jewish citizens—more than 20 percent of the recorded Jewish population in the U.S.S.R. in the 1959 census—listed Yiddish as their mother tongue. (Last year Soviet sources estimated that there must be some "three million Jews in the Soviet Union.")*

---

* As reported by the Soviet press agency Novosti. The results of a Soviet census of 1970, published in April 1971, speak of 2.15 million people who listed themselves as Jews.

"They are certainly entitled to more cultural attention than the publication of your literary monthly," I pointed out.

He admitted that there was still much to be done in the field of Jewish culture, and revealed that "something is being done experimentally in this direction." Among other things, his own magazine will introduce a special section to help students of the Yiddish language. He said that under the auspices of *Sovietish Heimland* two courses in Yiddish are to be established, one in Moscow and one in Leningrad.

"If this experiment works well, I will recommend the establishment of such courses in other cities as well," he declared. Each student will have to pay a small sum—a "symbolic payment"—to show that he is really interested in studying Yiddish, he added.

Sovietish Heimland, although a Communist-oriented publication, seems to be drifting more and more toward the publication of novels and poetry which are not saturated with Communist propaganda. Some of them are of high literary quality, written by a younger generation of Jewish writers, whom the magazine seeks to encourage. One can also find in the magazine selected items about Jewish literary events within the country and abroad.

Mr. Vergelis drew my attention to the fact that a Russian-Yiddish dictionary is now in preparation by the Soviet Jewish philologist, Moshe Shapiro, and will be published soon, as will a book on Yiddish grammar. He pointed out that about a half dozen Yiddish books—by living Soviet Jewish authors as well as by men killed by Stalin—appeared during the past year and can be found in all Soviet bookstores. Four of these books (by Z. Wendroff, Peretz Markish, Leib Kvitko, Moshe Teif) I actually saw prominently displayed in two Moscow bookshops specializing in books written in national minority languages.

All this is, of course, a welcome sign that literature in Yiddish is beginning to find its way again in the Soviet Union. But this is not enough, considering the number of Jews who declared Yiddish to be their mother tongue in the last census. A larger program conducted at a faster tempo is required if the Soviet authorities sincerely desire to show that they do not intend to discriminate against Jewish culture.

Soviet spokesmen, in discussing the position of Jewish culture in the U.S.S.R. today, admit that the Yiddish language can still be heard on the main streets of cities like Kiev, Odessa, Minsk, Riga, Vilna, Czernovitz, Kishinev, and even Moscow. However, they claim that those still speaking Yiddish are elderly Jews. The Jewish youth, they insist, do not speak or read Yiddish and do not even understand the language when they hear it spoken.

This is the excuse which Soviet officials give when asked why so little is being done now to restore Jewish culture to the level it reached prior to the years when all Jewish cultural institutions were done away with under Stalin. They refuse to accept the argument that the young generation of Jews has been alienated from the Yiddish language by the closing of all the Jewish schools and the complete liquidation, in 1948, of Jewish cultural life. They blame the Jewish parents for the demise of the Jewish schools. The parents, they say, preferred to send their children to general schools, where Russian is the language of instruction; hence there was no longer any need for the state to maintain Jewish schools.

They tell you frankly that under the present circumstances, when Jewish parents choose to send their children to a Russian-language school rather than to a school where the classes are conducted in Yiddish, they see no real motivation for re-opening the Jewish schools in any part of the country. They assert that a Jewish school system was established after the Revolution mainly because in those years Jewish children—especially in the small towns—felt more at home using Yiddish as their language and that this was primarily because under the Czarist regime a Jewish child was rarely accepted in a municipally supported school where education was conducted in the Russian language.

The situation began to change about fifteen years after the Revolution when Jewish youngsters shifted their interest from being educated in a Jewish school to receiving education in a general school, the Soviet officials say. By that time, they point out, the younger generation of Jews was speaking Russian freely. They felt themselves part and parcel of the country and had the doors of all the schools open to them without any discrimination. Many of them thus chose to receive their elementary education in the language of the land. In this they were encouraged by their parents, who believed that education in the Russian language would open wider possibilities for their children later on as regards higher study than would the available education in the Yiddish language. Today, thirty-five years later, all Jewish children everywhere in the country are eager to receive their education in Russian, the Soviet officials tell you, adding that they are skeptical as to whether in any Soviet city a Jewish school would have enough pupils for its classes.

The officials go out of their way to convince you that the decline of the use of Yiddish in the Soviet Union cannot be considered an indication that Jewish culture is being discriminated against in the country. They refer to the decline of Yiddish among native-born Jews in the United States, Britain, and France. They ignore, of course, the fact that Jewish schools, including religious all-day schools, still function freely and in substantial numbers in those countries.

To the question as to why the Soviet authorities do not permit the existence of at least Yiddish afternoon schools, or Sunday schools—as is the case in other countries—to supplement the education the Jewish children receive in Russian in the general school system, the Soviet officials reply that if a sufficient number of parents were interested in establishing such supplementary schools, they would probably find no obstacles in their way. They add that for those Jews who want to learn Yiddish, an acceptable form of learning might be provided by special courses or through study by correspondence.

In the opinion of Soviet spokesmen, Jewish culture is not only not suppressed in their country, but—on the contrary —is "flourishing and developing." They claim that through the Yiddish magazine *Sovietish Heimland* many new and young Yiddish novelists, essayists, literary critics, and poets have been developed during recent years. They refer to the huge successes of Yiddish concerts, to the production of recordings of Yiddish folksongs, to exhibitions of the work of

Jewish painters. They consider the publication of an anthology of modern Yiddish verse—which includes the works of fifty poets—a major event in Soviet Jewish literary life.

They also cite as a cultural achievement the fact that the works of Jewish authors are being published in Russian translation, and they point out that in 1965 a collection of stories by twenty-four Israeli writers was published in Moscow. This was followed a year later by the publication in Russian translation of short stories by twenty Israeli authors. There was also the publication of an anthology in Russian of contemporary Israeli verse, in which twenty poets are represented. These translated works, the Soviet officials maintain, are intended not only for the benefit of Soviet Jews who cannot read Yiddish or Hebrew—Hebrew is forbidden in the Soviet Union—but also for non-Jews who wish to become acquainted with Jewish literature.

In defending their views on the status of Jewish culture in their country, Soviet officials nevertheless feel uncomfortable when presented with the argument that all their enumerated efforts in the field of Jewish culture cannot cover the naked fact that Jewish education is nonexistent in the Soviet Union, even to the point where Jewish youths do not know their own history. There is no book on Jewish history to be bought in the Soviet Union—not even in the Russian language—despite the great surge among young Jews there to know the Jewish past.

The greatest spiritual hunger felt among Jews in the Soviet Union is for the Jewish theater and for Yiddish concerts.

Concerts by Jewish singers are given from time to time in Moscow, Leningrad, and other large cities, and they take place in the largest halls. They are always crowded. Tickets to such recitals are always sold out many days in advance. The programs of these concerts are mostly of Jewish folksongs of the prerevolutionary years. They strike a nostalgic chord in the hearts of older Jews as well as a sentimental chord among the younger Jews.

Jewish songs are so popular in the Soviet Union that some

Soviet opera singers include them in their concert programs. They draw tremendous applause. American singers, like Jan Peerce and Paul Robeson when giving concerts in Moscow, never fail to include a few popular Jewish songs, to the delight of the audience, which greets them with long-lasting, enthusiastic applause. At such concerts one can feel that the Jewish spirit is still strongly alive among Jews in Russia, assimilated or not.

Jews in the Soviet Union are also hungry for performances in Yiddish on the stage. There are a few wandering Jewish amateur groups which travel from city to city, performing Jewish plays in a primitive way. But there is no Jewish state theater like those that existed in Moscow, Kiev, and other large cities prior to Stalin's liquidation of Jewish culture.

I was informed in Moscow that a group of twenty-three young Jewish artists have been selected and are now being trained under the directorship of Benjamin Schwartzer, a veteran Jewish actor, with a view to eventually establishing a permanent Jewish theater in the Soviet capital. The theater, I was told, will be named either after Sholom Aleichem, the great Jewish writer who died in New York, or after Solomon Mikhoels, the great Soviet Yiddish actor who was killed by Stalin. However, this seems to be a long-term project which could not materialize in less than a year or two because of the length of the training the young actors require.

Time will show whether this project will be carried out and to what extent the Soviet Government will be interested in promoting it. Judging from the crowded halls at Jewish concerts and at the performances given by the traveling Jewish amateur groups, the need for a permanent Jewish state theater in Moscow, Kiev, Odessa, and other cities with a substantial Jewish population is immediate.

In the meantime, the outstanding Soviet Jewish songstress of Yiddish folksongs, Nechama Lifshitz, who took audiences by storm in every city where she appeared, left the Soviet Union in 1969 with the permission of the Soviet Government and settled in Israel. Her absence from the Soviet Union will mean a great loss for Soviet Jews longing for Jewish culture. She kept

Jewish nostalgic feelings alive with her concerts. Her emigration is indicative of the mood among those elements of Soviet Jewry who feel that the Soviet Government is not inclined to encourage the resurgence of Jewish culture in the country. She had the greatest success in her Yiddish repertoire, despite the Soviet claim that Yiddish is dying in Russia.

The fact that she was permitted to leave the Soviet Union for Israel at a time when no diplomatic relations exist between the two countries would have been welcomed under normal circumstances as a gesture of good will toward Jews on the part of the Soviet authorities. Under the existing circumstances, however, when the revival of Jewish culture in the Soviet Union needs such talents as Mrs. Lifshitz very badly, her departure can only be interpreted as tragic proof that even she, whom the Soviet authorities always mentioned as evidence that there is no suppression of Jewish culture in Russia, had good grounds to seek emigration. It also serves as indication that the Soviet Government is not interested in keeping even the remnants of Jewish culture at full strength, not to speak of developing new strength.

♦ ♦ ♦ 8

Jews in the Soviet Economy

On nevski prospect—Leningrad's Fifth Avenue —you read "help wanted" signs in the windows of practically every enterprise. Whether it is a shoe store or a cafe, a clothing store or a bakery, a bookstore or a grocery—everywhere there are vacancies for employment. Needed are bookkeepers and cashiers, typists and clerks, salesgirls and floor managers, waiters and cooks, dishwashers and floor cleaners.

On the side streets, at entrances to artisan shops and industrial enterprises, you see large posters announcing that all kinds of skilled workers and craftsmen are sought: mechanics, plumbers, steamfitters, electricians, machine operators—all the way to tailors and shoemakers. And again—bookkeepers, cashiers, and office workers.

You can see the same in Moscow, where cooperative stores, government department stores, small factories, and even drugstores display handwritten announcements offering jobs to both qualified and unqualified workers. This is true also in Kiev and in any of the larger cities in the Soviet Union. There is a shortage of labor today all over the Soviet Union.

In Kiev, on the Krestshatik—the most beautiful avenue, reminiscent of the Champs Élysées in Paris—the street in the area of the large central post office is being paved. Who is doing the paving? Red Army soldiers. Why soldiers? Because there are not enough civilian laborers to do the job.

Every few minutes military trucks are arriving with soldiers in their fatigues who lose no time in starting to shovel gravel and pour tar. There are also civilians sharing the work with them, but these are mostly middle-aged women of the peasant type who are usually the street cleaners of the city. The paving must be completed by a certain time, and without the help of soldiers as workers the schedule will not be accomplished. There are not enough men willing to do the heavy and dirty work of paving the street. Men can get better-paid jobs even if they have no special qualifications.

Unlike in the United States, Soviet newspapers print no "want ads." If they did, the newspapers in the larger cities would have pages and pages of them. The country is now undergoing a tremendous upsurge in various branches of heavy industry and in housing building. There is also a growth in light industry, providing articles for home consumption which had not been produced for many years. The shortage in labor is therefore not surprising.

Jews in the Soviet Union, when they look for work now, have, therefore, no difficulty in finding it, whether in offices or factories. Their identity documents, marking them as Jews, no longer stand in the way of their being employed, as was the case a few years ago, even in the Khrushchev period.

There was a time when one of the popular jokes in the Soviet Union was about a Jew applying for a job in a factory. The personnel manager examined his application and told him: "Sorry, you are in the wrong place. We are not in the nuclear power industry!" The implication of the joke was that Jews are given jobs only in the field of atomic science, where they are needed because of their higher education and special knowledge, but not in ordinary work in stores, factories, and offices.

This is not the case today. All jobs are open to them because workers and other employees are needed everywhere in the large cities. They may not be promoted in their jobs because of their Jewish identity, but they are no longer refused employment.

It is difficult to establish the number of Jews now working in Soviet industry, although each industrial enterprise in the country knows exactly how many Jews it carries on its payroll. The records in Soviet enterprises—whether industrial or commercial—indicate the nationality of each employee, whether he is a Jew, a Russian, a Ukrainian, or a native of any other Soviet republic in the U.S.S.R.

In small provincial towns, where there are no industrial enterprises, the finding of a proper job is still a problem for Jews. Jews in the small towns are primarily artisans working in cooperatives, or are engaged in "white-collar" professions.

My attempts in Moscow to proceed to small provincial towns to look into the economic situation of Jews there were not successful. Soviet authorities do not permit foreigners to visit even the larger provincial cities like Berdichev, Zhitomir, Rovno, and others, which were known for their large Jewish populations in the prewar years. You are told in Moscow that there are few Jews there now because the Germans killed all the Jews there during the occupation period. You are also told that there are no hotels in these cities for foreigners to stay in comfortably. At any rate, you are discouraged by the Moscow authorities from going there and are not permitted to proceed into the provincial places you want to visit. You are thus prevented from looking into the Jewish situation on the spot.

Jews coming from some of the provincial towns to Moscow tell you, however, that it is very difficult for a Jew to get a position in a municipal office, especially in the Ukraine, where it is almost impossible for a Jew to become a clerk even in a post office. At the same time they tell you that they are more or less satisfied with their lot as far as "making a living" goes. They limit their complaints more to cultural "starvation" than to economic deprivation.

Take the case of Solomon Davidovich Kagan, a Jewish worker who is not a member of the Communist Party.

When I knew him in Moscow in the 1930's, he was manager of a state garage. There were very few taxis in Moscow at that time, but I never had any difficulty getting one whenever needed. All I had to do was to telephone the garage and ask him to send a taxi to pick me up. This was done by him always in sincere friendship. I lived in a cooperative house built by engineers, one of whom was his brother, who was later transferred to the Urals.

I met him now quite incidentally when I was standing in front of the Metropole Hotel in Moscow looking for a taxi. One of the Intourist cab drivers who are always stationed near the hotel awaiting assignments from the Intourist office came over to me.

"Look who is here!" he exclaimed with affection. "Why, if it is not Mr. Smolar!"

I must admit that I did not recognize him. Quite a number of years have passed since I saw him last. In the meantime there was a war in which he fought at the front. I did not change much in appearance during the years, but he did. When I knew him he was a man of about forty; now he was an aged person of over sixty-five. He was robust, looked healthy, but was quite gray.

He realized that I did not recognize him and came to my assistance. "Remember my brother? . . . Remember the taxis I used to send you from the garage? . . . Remember Arbatskaya Ploshchad?"

Arbatskaya Ploshchad was the neighborhood where I lived and where his taxis used to pick me up. How could I forget it? Those taxis were my lifesavers when I was in a hurry to reach the censor at the Foreign Office at Kuznetsky Most, many blocks away, in a city where a taxi was a rarity.

"You are not Solomon Davidovich?" I hesitated to indicate that I did not recognize him.

"The very same!" he acknowledged cheerfully. "The very same, but much older. Years, as you know, have a tradition of not standing still. They also have a habit of leaving a mark on a person, especially when one has lived through what we have lived through since I saw you last. Although you have not changed much during those years, I know that I have changed a lot. No wonder you did not recognize me at the first look."

Old friendship restored, he introduced me to the other taxi drivers who were awaiting assignments.

"He lived in my brother's home before the war," he told his group about me. "He is an American who talks Russian. I used to dispatch taxis to him from our garage when I was manager." There was a friendly boasting tone in this introduction.

He wanted to know whether I was staying at the Metropole Hotel, how long I was going to stay in the Soviet Union this time, whether I had come alone or with my wife, and showered me with all kinds of questions, like a long-lost relative. I, on the other hand, was hesitant to ask him any questions in front of the others who surrounded us, watching with great curiosity the enthusiasm he displayed so emotionally at our sudden reunion. All I managed to ask him was whether he was married by now.

"Of course I am married now!" he said in a tone of happiness. "Not only am I married, but I also now have two sons —one is a university student," he added proudly.

I wanted very much to ask him why he was no longer manager of a garage, but just an ordinary driver. However, I controlled myself from asking this delicate question in front of his colleagues. Figuring that while in his taxi I would be able to ask him this and other questions more freely, I told him that I was looking for a taxi and wanted to know whether he could take me to my destination despite the fact that I was not entitled to the use of an Intourist car.

"Where do you want to go?" He was eager to accommodate me.

"To the American Embassy," was my reply.

He thought for a moment and then said: "I'll have to check it with the manager of the Intourist taxi fleet at the hotel. I am certain he will have no objection when I tell him that I knew you years ago. It is merely a matter of formality. He has to know where I am going."

He disappeared for a few minutes and came back all smiles.

"It's all right," he said. "I can take you wherever you want to go and for as long as you want to go. I can even wait for you, should this be necessary. The manager was very understanding. I am entirely at your disposal. But better watch my meter. Taxi rides are not expensive in Moscow, but the total on the meter can be very substantial on long rides."

During the ride I posed to him the question which was on my mind. Had he been demoted from manager of a state garage to ordinary taxi driver? Was there any reason for the change in his position? Was it because he was Jewish? Was it because he was not a member of the Communist Party?

He listened to me attentively and smiled.

"No," he said. "I was not demoted. When I returned from the front at the end of the war I was welcomed back to my old job. You must understand that since the years when you knew me as garage manager in charge of a few rickety taxis, Moscow has become a city of thousands of automobiles and many hundreds of taxis. Also, that I am a skilled mechanic who can get a very good job in any factory. It is not I who needed my old job. On the contrary—the job needed me. I drove a tank during the war and distinguished myself on the battlefront. Neither my being a Jew nor my not being a party member was held against me. I returned to my former position of manager of a taxi fleet as a decorated war veteran.

"It was when I reached my retirement age that I decided to become just a simple taxi driver. I was put on a proper pension when I reached the age of sixty, and I am continuing to get this pension. However, there is an acute shortage of taxi drivers. So I decided to earn additional income by working voluntarily as a taxi driver, putting in as much time as I choose. I could have continued to hold the managerial position and get a salary in addition to my pension, but that would have meant that I have to put in a full day's work. As a supernumerary taxi driver I am under no obligation as to working hours. I work whenever I feel like and as many hours as I like. I work because I feel strong enough to work and because too much leisure would bore me. But I do not want to overwork at my age. Hence I took to taxi driving on a per hour basis."

Does he feel there is discrimination against Jews in his field of work?

He thought for a few seconds and said: "In my field of work there is hardly any discrimination. Firstly, because you find few Jews among taxi drivers. If a Jew is mechanically minded he prefers to work in industrial enterprises. And secondly because, as I have already told you, there is a great shortage of cab drivers. In other fields of work Jews complain that they are not being promoted to higher positions, but this does not apply to the field of cab driving. A taxi driver does not expect promotions. Besides, you may find Jews in garages as mechanics and managers—again because there is a shortage in that category of employees. Jew or no Jew—the administration does not want to lose any of its employees. This is also the case today in factories, in offices, and in any field of employment. Workers and employees are now needed everywhere, and the Jew is just as good a worker as the non-Jew. In many cases he proves to be even better. There are practically no drunkards among Jews, and this means that there is no absenteeism from work among Jews on jobs—a matter which counts very much in favor of an employee in our country."

Naturally we also spoke about our family lives and he told me that his wife was not Jewish, but this did not in the least affect their home life. His children knew that they were Jewish because of their last name and also because he subscribes to *Sovietish Heimland.*

"I still like to look into something printed in Yiddish. But Russian is our family language," he said. "My wife does not know any language except Russian and this is also the case with my two sons. They were brought up in Russian and this is their mother tongue." It was obvious from his conversation that his children know nothing about Jewishness and that their Jewish identity means nothing to them.

Somewhat contrary is the case of Alexander Levin, also a Jew and also not a member of the Communist Party.

Levin is an engineer, one of the many thousands of engineers engaged in building Soviet industry in all parts of the country. Because of his proven ability, he is the director of a factory producing electrical equipment. He is dedicated to his work, gets along well with his staff and with his workers, and is producing more than the quota which his factory has been assigned under a scheduled plan.

In his personal life he has nothing to complain about. He is satisfied with his salary, lives with his wife and two children in a newly built apartment house, has a television set and a refrigerator in his home, has a record player along with a library of good records of classical music, and even enjoys the use of a car which is part of the factory's inventory.

Yet he is not entirely happy. He feels he is lacking recognition on the part of his higher authorities.

"You see," he confided in me as in a friend, "many in my position have received decorations for the performance of the factories which they supervise. I have not even received a citation for the excellent record which our factory enjoys as far as production and quality are concerned. It hurts when you think of it. It also undermines one's status with the workers."

"Do you think that this is due to the fact that you are not a member of the Communist Party, or to the fact that you are a Jew, or maybe to both?" I asked him.

He was not sure. Directors of other factories have been awarded decorations despite the fact that they are not members of the Communist Party. As a non-Communist he would long ago have been replaced in his position had his record of production not been so high and had he not been so popular with the workers in his factory. The fact that he has never been moved from his position is the best testimony in favor of his record.

"Then it must be that your Jewish identity stands in the way of your being awarded the deserved decoration," I ventured to speculate.

"I don't know," was his measured reply. "I am reluctant to think that this is the cause, and yet you may be right. You see, there are many Jewish engineers and factory directors who have received special honorary titles for the service they rendered. But these are all people of the older generation. There have been few such honors awarded during the last few years except to outstanding Jewish scientists. You begin to develop an inferiority complex when you see others in your class being honored by the government while you are ignored despite your devotion."

There was a feeling of pain in his observations. Ever since his student years he had not thought in terms of being a Jew, although his identity documents indicated his Jewish nationality. He was raised in an assimilated atmosphere. In the factory which he manages there were workers of various nationalities and his office staff included numerous Jews as clerks, typists, bookkeepers. But he never paid any attention to the nationality of any of the employees. He considered himself—and still considers himself—a part of the Soviet people. The suspicion that among his superiors there may be some who are influenced by the fact that he is a Jew makes him feel that something is wrong somewhere. Not with him, but with the people above him who are in a position to make decisions affecting his fate.

He is not afraid that he may lose his position. The Soviet economy needs engineers badly. He will always be a part of the Soviet economic and industrial machine whether he holds his present post or is transferred to another. And this seems to be the feeling today of most of the Jews in the Soviet Union. They are all needed by the growing Soviet economy— whether they are industrial workers, construction workers, or even unskilled workers.

You visit Soviet factories and you now find there Jewish proficient welders, laborers, fitters, technicians, and even foremen. In Soviet state stores you can find Jewish saleswomen and cashiers. In the Intourist offices in Moscow and Leningrad—but not in Kiev—you can see quite a number of Jewish girls working at information desks and as typists. In the banks you find Jewish girls both as clerks and as cashiers. In the shops you find Jewish salesgirls. You may even find Jewish girls among the Intourist guides, although this is considered a "sensitive" field of employment. Taking foreign tourists on excursions and explaining to them institutions or even localities is considered an important political function. The guide must be a politically trusted person and is expected to slant his explanations in accord with the official government line.

The Soviet economic machine, in need of all kinds of labor, no longer makes any distinction between Jew and non-Jew, as was the case during the latter years of the Stalin regime, or even in the early years of the Khrushchev regime. Promotion of Jews to higher positions is a different thing. This may explain why some Jewish engineers, even when they reach the point of occupying managerial posts in which they distinguish themselves, feel that they do not receive the same recognition they see given to others.

I have seen lists of Jews who were awarded decorations and medals for their contributions to Soviet science and industry. But these were all scientists who contributed something new and important in the field of thermonuclear science, in the field of higher mathematics, in the field of electric energy, and in the field of technical scholarship. In the Soviet Union today Jews excel in science, in research, and in inventions. This is recognized by all who watch Soviet industries growing and Soviet science reaching new heights. Yet, few such Jews are publicly appreciated. The majority of them remain "unknown soldiers" on the fronts of science and industry. Alexander Levin is one of the latter.

♦ ♦ ♦ 9

Jewish Generals, Admirals, and Scientists in the Soviet Union

On a sunny afternoon, at the end of April 1960, I received a telephone call in New York from the White House. James C. Hagerty, President Eisenhower's press secretary, was on the phone.

"You know about the forthcoming meeting in Moscow between President Eisenhower and Soviet Premier Nikita Khrushchev," he said. "We are now completing the preparations for the President's trip. Would you like to join the group of journalists accompanying the President?"

"I will consider it a great honor!" was my reply.

"Then mail me your passport. We will get your visa from the Soviet Embassy here."

It occurred to me to ask whether it could be arranged that the Soviet visa would permit me also to stay over for a fortnight in the Soviet Union after the departure of President Eisenhower from Moscow.

"I am interested in looking into the situation of Soviet Jewry," I explained. "During the Eisenhower-Khrushchev summit talks there will be no time left for me to make an effort in this direction. However, after the official meeting is over and the President's party leaves Moscow, it would be most important for me to remain there, and also to visit other Soviet cities, in order to get an authentic picture of how the Jews live in the Soviet Union under Khrushchev as compared with the terror they have undergone during the last years of Stalin's life."

"I am sure it can be arranged!" was Hagerty's reply.

I was elated over the invitation to join the Presidential party and over the opportunity to get first-hand information on the "Jewish problem" in the Soviet Union, both from Jews there as well as from high government officials whom I planned to approach. I started to make the arrangements for the trip.

Shortly after the first of May I received another telephone call from Washington, from Mr. Hagerty's office:

"You probably know what happened! . . . The President's trip is canceled! . . ."

What happened is now a part of history in American-Soviet relations. An American U-2 "spy plane" was shot down over Soviet territory near Sverdlovsk, in the Ural Mountains, on the eve of President Eisenhower's trip to Moscow. Khrushchev was infuriated that such a plane, equipped to take pictures of Soviet sensitive military installations from a very high altitude, was sent by the Central Intelligence Agency just at the time when he was preparing to give President Eisenhower an elaborate reception in Moscow. He lost no time informing Washington that because of the U-2 incident, President Eisenhower's visit to the Soviet capital would not be welcome. The planned Eisenhower-Khrushchev meeting in Moscow was thus canceled.

The news of the bringing down of the U-2 plane was hailed throughout the Soviet Union as an example of the great achievements in Soviet military science. And an outstanding achievement it was, considering the height from which it was shot down and even the fact that the plane was detected at such height. But the Soviet people, while celebrating the feat, were not told by their government that this feat was achieved due to two Jewish men in the Soviet military aviation service. Nor was the world told about it.

Seven years later, in 1967, a Soviet military publication *Voyenno-Istoricheski Zhurnal* ("The Military-History Journal") revealed the names of the two men in an article in its October issue, entitled "Guarding the Soviet Sky." In this specialized magazine, the existence of which is not even known to the average civilian in the Soviet Union, a military expert, Major B. Zabelok, writing on the destruction by Soviet rockets of the U-2 plane, gave credit for this act to Lieutenant E. E. Feldblum and Sergeant B. Shuster—both Jews—for spotting the American plane on radar at very great heights. He called their achievement "a masterful piece of work."

Why did the Soviet press keep the names of the two Jewish men hidden all the time when it jubilantly reported many details of the shooting down of the American plane as an example of the success of the Soviet defense system? . . . Why were these names brought out only seven years later and only in an obscure military publication which does not reach the wide public? . . .

The answer is that while Jews play a very important role in the development of Soviet airspace and atomic science and rocketry, the Soviet Government is not interested in making this fact widely known to the Soviet population.

The deposed Premier Khrushchev, when asked about Soviet discrimination against Jews at a luncheon tendered to him in September 1959, in Washington, at the National Press Club, declared that among the persons who were taking the "foremost part in launching our rocket to the moon, Jews held a place of honor!" He thereby meant to indicate that Jews are not entirely eliminated from sensitive positions in his country. However, inside the Soviet Union no such statements have ever been made by any Soviet leader. The average Soviet citizen is thus not aware of the important role which Jewish scientists play in the development of the Soviet lunar venicles and in extending Soviet atomic power.

In the city of Dubno, in the Ukraine, which is one of the major centers of Soviet nuclear science, there are quite a large number of Jews among the scientists working in the laboratories there. Seldom does one come across the name of any of them in the Soviet press, although a good many of them have been decorated for their contributions to Soviet science and technology, as I have established. The same is true with regard to Soviet institutions of atomic science concentrated in certain parts of Siberia. Similar is the situation with Soviet airspace installations in Kazakhstan, Soviet Asia, where Jews constitute a substantial percentage of those working there on the development of missiles and "sputniks."

The Soviet press agency Novosti—which specializes in dissemination of news and articles in countries outside the Soviet Union—reported in 1963 that there were 36,173 Jewish scientists, constituting about 9 percent of the total scientists in the country. But this report was not disseminated to the press within the Soviet Union.

It is estimated that of the total Lenin Prizes for science and technology, about 10 percent are awarded to Jewish scientists. But don't look in the Soviet press for names of the Jewish recipients of this highest award. Here and there you may find in *Pravda* or in *Izvestia* names of Jewish scientists whose reputation is all too well known to ignore them, but this is an exception to the rule. The rule is to overlook the role which Jews play in the development of various forms of military and technological science.

On the other hand, the Soviet authorities make public fully the names of Jews awarded orders and decorations for their contributions in the fields of music, art, journalism, and medicine. In these fields, too, the Jews play an important role, although many of the journalists prefer to write not under their own names, but under a non-Jewish-sounding pen name.

In Moscow, at Neglinnaya Street 29/14, there is the seat of the government committee which recommends the bestowal of Lenin Prizes and other government awards in the fields of science and technology. The committee is headed by Professor M. Keldish, member of the Academy of Sciences of the U.S.S.R. and one of the outstanding Soviet men of science.

You are presented there with a list of scientific papers which have been endorsed in 1967 for state prizes of the year by scholars, scientific institutions, and even Soviet ministries. The list of subjects with which the papers deal is impressive. They embrace nuclear energy, aviation, geophysics, geochemistry, aerophotography, telemechanics, metallurgy, automation, and numerous other newly developed theories in various sciences based on research and experiments.

Jewish names stand out very conspicuously in the list. I counted seventy-two of them. It is possible that among the approximately two hundred candidates listed for the Lenin Prize and other prizes were even more than the seventy-two whose names are Jewish without any doubt. Some Jewish scientists in the Soviet Union can be mistaken for non-Jewish because their names do not sound Jewish. The names I picked from the list were typically Jewish, like I. Lemberg, A. Grinberg, M. Temkin, F. Wolfson, I. Ginsburg, M. Levin, G. Bruk, L. Minz, M. Eidelman, M. Rosenblat, A. Goldman, B. Zusman, M. Goldstein, I. Shifrin, Y. Segalovich, L. Rosenberg, and numerous other such conspicuously Jewish names.

This gives an idea of the contributions Jews make in the Soviet Union in the field of high scholarship. Not all on the list —which concerned the best-selected contributions of the year—will receive the coveted prizes, but some of them undoubtedly will. Whether this recognition will be made public to the people of the country is doubtful, since this would clash with the government policy of subduing the services which Jews perform in the most vital fields of science.

Studying Soviet military records, as well as the Official Gazette of each of the fifteen Soviet Republics, one is especially impressed with the role which Jews play in aviation.

Under the present Soviet policy, Jews no longer hold high-ranking offices as was the case with Air Marshal Yakov Smushkevich who was "liquidated" by Stalin in 1941. You read the orders of the Supreme Soviet awarding high military decorations to Jewish aviators and trainers of pilots for their extraordinary services but among those so honored, none is higher than the rank of captain. There have been no promotions for Jews to higher military ranks since the years when Stalin removed many Jewish generals and colonels from their positions.

Some ten years ago, Lieutenant General David Dragunsky, a Jew upon whom the title "Hero of the Soviet Union"—the highest military decoration—was conferred twice, spoke of "hundreds of Jewish generals and admirals in the Soviet Union." At a press interview, he mentioned three: the Supreme Commander in the Far East, the commander of the Military Academy, and the commander of a defense force on the southern border. Today one can still find a Jewish general here and there in the Soviet armed forces, but primarily in the medical and engineering corps. In 1970 General Dragunsky participated in a government-sponsored press conference in Moscow at which he denounced Zionism and Soviet Jews who want to leave for Israel. At the end of 1970 he also visited the Latin American countries on a mission to deny Soviet discrimination against Jews. General Dragunsky also appeared in Brussels at the end of February 1971 at a pro-Soviet meeting aimed at counteracting a three-day world Jewish conference on Soviet Jewry held during that week in Brussels at which the restoration of full rights for Jews in the Soviet Union was demanded as well as the reunification of Soviet Jews with members of their families abroad. General Dragunsky came all the way from Moscow to address the apologetic pro-Soviet meeting as the principal speaker.

The two best known Jewish admirals during World War II were Rear Admiral Semyon Yurovsky and Rear Admiral Paul Trainin. Nobody knows their whereabouts now. The "liquidated" Air Force Marshal Smushkevich was "rehabilitated" in 1963, twenty-two years after his execution. Today one reads articles about him in the Soviet press glorifying his military achievements and telling the story of how he, a Lithuanian Jew, joined the Red Army in 1918, at the age of sixteen; how he distinguished himself during World War II in commanding the air force on the Leningrad front and other fronts; how he was decorated twice with the highest military award "Hero of the Soviet Union"; and how he organized the air force in Spain for the anti-Franco fighters during the civil war.

Similar articles with high praise appear now from time to time for other "liquidated" Jewish generals who were posthumously rehabilitated in the post-Stalin years. Photographs are now being reprinted in Soviet publications not only of Marshal Smushkevich but also of other Soviet Jewish generals who had "disappeared" during the late years of the Stalin regime. They include General Grigory Shtern who commanded the Red Army forces in the Far East in 1938, defeating the Japanese military attempts there, and who died mysteriously in 1940; Army General Lev Mekhlis who served as Deputy Commissar of Defense and was discarded in 1950; Major General Lev Dovator, commander of the Red Cavalry Corps who was a heroic military figure; General Matvei Wainrub, who as commander of tank forces played an important role in winning the battle at Stalingrad and later commanded the armor in the final offensive on Berlin in 1945.

In 1956 the name of Colonel General Yakov Kreizer was mentioned by Khrushchev, the then Soviet Premier. He said that General Kreizer, "a good friend of mine and a Jew," served somewhere near Sverdlovsk, in the Ural Mountains. The Jewish general had commanded the Third Army in decisive battles for Moscow and later defeated the German Army in the Crimea, recapturing the port city of Sevastopol. He died in 1969.

While one finds now no reference to Jewish generals and even colonels in the Supreme Soviet orders for honors and awards, one comes across Jewish names of officers in the lower ranks when studying the lists of military decorations in the Official Gazette. One such recent list contains the names of Captain Grigory Kushnirov and Captain Paul Yuger, with emphasis by the Supreme Soviet that the two were being decorated for "special achievements" in the field of aviation and for "excellence" in training pilots and in building cadres of military fliers.

One of the outstanding Jewish fliers in the Soviet civil aviation system Aeroflot—about whom much is written in the

Soviet press—is Igor Benyaminovich Buzyka. He is commander of the giant "TU-114" flying the long distance between Moscow and Chabarovsk. He carries the modest title
"engineer-pilot."

A report on Jewish participation in World War II, issued
by Novosti in English and in French for information abroad,
says that about five hundred thousand Jews fought in the
ranks of the Soviet Army during the war and that 160,772 of
them were decorated for heroism and bravery. This puts the
Jews fourth in the ranks of war heroes after the Russians,
Ukrainians, and Byelorussians, and ahead of all other nationalities in the Soviet Union. It brings out vividly the role which
the Jews played on the fronts in the battles against the German Army.

Nevertheless in the Soviet volume *Outstanding Victories of
the Soviet Army in the Great War of Liberation*—published
in Russian—the number of Jewish war heroes is completely
omitted, although the data on each of the various other nationalities is given; even of those nationalities who received less
than three thousand decorations.

Similarly, while the Novosti report in English indicates that
114 Jews have been awarded the highest Soviet military
decoration—the title "Hero of the Soviet Union"—for the
part they played in crucial operations on the battlefront
against the Germans, this fact is omitted from a Soviet booklet
published by the State Publishing House in Moscow. No Jews
are listed in this booklet among those bestowed with the order
"Hero of the Soviet Union." The statistical breakdown by nationalities leaves out the Jews despite the fact that as recipients
of the "Hero of the Soviet Union" they rank the fifth as a nationality after the Russians, Ukrainians, Byelorussians, and
Tartars. The booklet appeared under the title "National Traditions of the Peoples of the Soviet Union."

There is no doubt about the great contribution which Jewish scientists and research men are making to the country. Although no publicity is given to this fact in the Soviet press, it
is nevertheless known—although not among the population
—that a Jew, Professor Hirsh Budker, holds the very impor-

tant position of Director of the Nuclear Physics Institute of the Soviet Academy of Sciences in Siberia. Another Jewish scientist, Alex Naumov, is deputy director of the same institute. In the Ukraine a Jewish scientist Ilya Lifshitz holds a similar important post of Director of Physics and Technology at the Institute of Academic Sciences in the Ukraine. All three of them are members of the Academy of Sciences of the U.S.S.R. and holders of the coveted Lenin Prize for their scientific achievements.

Soviet official documents indicate that more than thirty Jewish scholars in the field of nuclear physics, chemistry, and technology have been awarded high decorations in 1967. They included the two eminent chemists Alexander Frumkin and Semion Wolfkovich, who are members of the U.S.S.R. Academy of Sciences. About twenty Jewish names could be found in the list of candidates to fill vacancies in 1966 of forty-one members and fifty-three corresponding members of the Academy of Sciences, most of them for the department of nuclear physics, general physics, and applied physics. Eleven of them, all professors, were elected. Of the more than two hundred members of the Academy and about four hundred corresponding members, reported in *Novoye Vremya* of 1967, about 10 percent are Jewish, in addition to about twenty Jews who are members and corresponding members of the Academy of Medical Sciences.

All this is known to a limited number of people in the Soviet Union. The Soviet authorities cannot keep the fact of Jewish participation in the development of science totally unknown, but prefer to leave out wherever possible any indication of the great contribution which Soviet Jews make to the basic sciences.

The year 1967 was perhaps a year in which the largest number of honors and awards were conferred upon civilians in the Soviet Union. It was the fiftieth year of the October Revolution which brought the Lenin regime to power. Official Soviet data—dated October 28, 1967—an order of the Presidium of the Supreme Soviet—reveals that a total of 128,657 orders and medals were bestowed in that year upon active participants in the first five years of the October Revolution. You study the lists of the decorated and you find only 670 Jews there with 366 of them decorated in Leningrad. It is obvious that there were more than 304 Jews outside of Leningrad who actively participated in the building of the Soviet system during the first five years of the regime, although many of them have since died and others were "liquidated" in the last years of Stalin's life.

♦ ♦ ♦ IO

Among Jewish Students
at Moscow University

SOVIET SCHOOLS OF HIGHER LEARNING carry exact
data on the number of their Jewish students. You can ask the
administration of the Moscow University how many Jewish
students are registered there and you will be given the information within a few minutes if doing so is in the Soviet interest. Especially is this true if the officials want to convince you
that there is no anti-Jewish discrimination in the admission of
students.

Under the Soviet system the record of each student must indicate his nationality. Thus, every university, or any other
school of higher learning, can easily establish how many of its
students are of Russian, Ukrainian, Jewish, Byelorussian, or
other nationality. Soviet officials tell you that according to
their data there are today about ninety-five thousand Jewish
students in establishments of higher education and that this
comes to about three hundred students per ten thousand of the
Jewish population in the country. They stress the fact that this
is a much higher proportion in comparison with the other nationalities. The average number of students for the entire pop-

ulation in the Soviet Union is about 165 per ten thousand of
the population, they assert.

You cite the fact that the proportion of Jewish students is,
nevertheless, much smaller today than it was in the thirties,
when Jews knew of no restrictions in any sector of Soviet life.
You get the answer that since then the ratio of rural-to-urban
population has changed, with the concomitant result that an
increased number of youngsters (other than Jewish) who for-
merly lived in culturally backward rural communities have
begun to seek university education. This, Soviet officials explain, has automatically reduced the proportion of Jewish students.

You are presented with data showing that 96 percent of the
Jewish population are today city and town dwellers. This, you
are told, is the reason there are now about three hundred students to each ten thousand Jews in the country. Your attention is drawn to figures showing that among Ukrainians—
who have a large proportion of village population—there
are only about 150 students in higher education for each ten
thousand persons, and that even among Russians the proportion is only about 185 per ten thousand, because a large proportion of Russians live in villages and small towns.

You are told that the number of Jewish specialists with
higher and specialized secondary education who are employed
in the Soviet national economy has increased annually during
recent years and is now close to five hundred thousand. You
are also told that today 14 percent of the total Jewish population of the country have a higher or specialized secondary education, whereas the average number of the same category of
educated persons in the country totals only about 5 percent of
the entire population.

All this data is presented to you by the Soviet officials in
refutation of the argument that restrictions are being applied
quietly in Soviet universities with regard to the admission of
Jews as students. But what is the factual situation? What does
an impartial observer establish when he visits a Soviet university? What have Jewish students themselves to say about their

status in the university? What have the Jewish faculty members to say?

A visit to Moscow University and frank talks there with groups of Jewish students—and with some of the faculty members—gave me an insight into the "Jewish moods" prevailing there.

There is no doubt that there is a tendency on the part of the Soviet Government quietly to curtail Jewish ambitions for higher education and to encourage a larger proportion of non-Jews to enter universities. This is especially true in the Ukraine, Byelorussia, and the other Soviet Republics where nationalism is strong and where the non-Jewish population is comparatively less educated on the average than the Jewish.

However, the Soviet Union, with its expanding industry and the great lack of engineers, physicists, chemists, and other experts in modern science, can hardly afford to discriminate against anyone who is a potential asset to the industrial development of the country or to its military machine. Thus Jews are now playing an important role as engineers in factories, in mines, in shipbuilding, as well as in the production of nuclear weapons, in sending satellites to the moon, and in all branches of atomic science. They are also very visible in the field of medicine, both as practicing physicians and in medical research.

You enter the premises of Moscow University and you see quite a number of students whom you can recognize as Jews. In addition, there are many Jewish students who do not look like Jews at all. There is very little difference today in appearance between Jewish and non-Jewish youth in Moscow. Also in the behavior. There are generally no anti-Jewish feelings among non-Jewish students on the campus. There is a normal relationship there with no visible signs of distinction between Jew and non-Jews. In fact, there is a great deal of intermarriage between students.

You talk to students and they are very frank in answering your questions. From their answers a picture emerges indicating that in some classes you can find quite a satisfactory number of Jewish students while in other classes the number is not so satisfactory. They are, on the average, of the opinion that one can find plenty of Jewish students in Soviet schools of higher education, but that there is a "selective" system prevailing in some of these schools—between admitting a Jewish applicant and a non-Jewish applicant of the same preparation, preference is usually given to the non-Jew.

The group of Jewish students with whom I was discussing their problems on the grounds of the university was aware of the fact that I was a foreigner. I introduced myself at the very beginning of our conversation as an American Jew, in order not to involve any one of the group in possible difficulties for talking to a foreigner. I spoke to them in Russian and each of the students understood me and could have left the premises without participating in the discussion. However, all remained around me although I was pointedly direct in my first question.

"Do you believe that discrimination is being practiced by the University against Jewish applicants seeking admission?"

A girl student, probably the most courageous of the group, exchanged looks with other students, obviously seeking their approval for what she was going to answer, and said: "If you were to enter my classroom you would find that a very substantial percentage of the students are Jews. In fact, quite a large percentage. However, that is because we are needed and not because we are wanted. Our class happens to be a class for higher mathematics, and when it comes to higher mathematics we Jews excel as compared with other students. Some non-Jewish students do not even want to register for this subject because it is a most difficult subject to study. But the country needs students of higher mathematics. So here we are."

She looked mischievously at the other students around her, received from them a smile indicating approval, and continued: "We are admitted because of our brains and because the country needs our scientific knowledge. In other faculties, however, you will not find many Jews. In classes of political science, the graduates of which are later given government political positions, you will probably not find any Jew."

She spoke her mind openly and was encouraged by the silent smiling of the students around her. It is a fact that in classes on nuclear physics and higher mathematics Jewish students stand more chance of being accepted because they face little competition. This explains why the number of Jewish scientists in the Soviet nuclear industry is substantial to a point that when he visited the United States even Khrushchev admitted Jewish participation in enabling the sending of Soviet satellites to circle the globe. This also explains why about sixty Jews are members and corresponding members of the U.S.S.R. Academy of Sciences, to which only outstanding scientists are elected.

While in the fields of higher mathematics, engineering, and medicine Jews have a better chance than in other fields— both as students and, later on, in practical application of their knowledge—because the country needs them, the situation is different in other fields of study.

An instructor at Moscow University, a young Jew who has been teaching the history of Russian literature—and who has few Jewish students in his classes—reluctantly gave me a picture of how things are for Jews in faculties not engaged in teaching science.

"I have been on the university's teaching staff for more than five years," he said. "But I do not think that I have a chance to reach a professorship soon, or even to become an assistant professor. It is more than four years since I submitted my doctoral thesis, but I have not been summoned as yet to defend it. Thus, I have not even received my doctorate, and who knows when I will ever receive it. My submitted thesis lies in a drawer somewhere and is not being moved. In the meantime, I am teaching my subject as an instructor."

The young man is certain that were he not a Jew he would have received his doctorate long ago and would by now have been well on his way to a professorship.

"There is no hurry in the Soviet Union today to give the

professorship title to a Jew, unless he distinguishes himself in atomic science," he mutters, as if speaking to himself. He is nevertheless optimistic. He believes that the day will come when he will receive his doctorate. He is an expert on Russian literature—old and new—and is very much liked by his students, who are mostly non-Jews and who find it easier to study the history of literature than higher mathematics or medicine.

Soviet authorities, in seeking to impress you with the argument that no anti-Jewish bias is being applied in schools of higher learning, also point to the fact that the number of Jews engaged in research work is increasing rather than decreasing every year. They estimate that more than fifty thousand Jews are now doing research work in various fields. They tell you that the number of Ukrainians engaged in research work is only about seventy thousand at a time when there are thirteen times as many Ukrainians in the Soviet Union as there are Jews. Here they prefer to omit the fact that at least two-thirds of the Ukrainians are village people whose education is very limited

The general impression one gets after talking with all parties involved is that Jewish students find their way into Soviet universities but the tendency of the authorities is to hold their number down wherever possible. The fact that Jewish students must state their nationality on their applications for admission to schools of higher learning—as must students of all other nationalities—makes it easier for the university administrations to check their number and for university authorities to choose between admitting them or applicants of other nationalities with equal marks in entrance examinations.

As matters stand now no Jewish applicant is certain that he will be admitted even if he passes with higher marks than a non-Jewish applicant. A certain percentage of Jewish students will always be found in Soviet universities, but the percentage may gradually become smaller with every year because of the official view that place must be made for youths who are leaving the rural localities where they were born and moving to cities to get a higher education. Does this mean outright discrimination against Jews? Perhaps not. However, it does mean that quietly a restrictive quota for Jews exists in schools of higher education and will probably continue to exist as long as the word "Jew" on the applicant's registration form provides an easy means to exclude him.

Mixed Marriages in the Soviet Union

THE YOUNG MAN IN KIEV who volunteered to take me to Babi Yar—the ravine where the Nazis machine-gunned tens of thousands of Kiev Jews in 1941, in cold blood —was a half-Jew. His father was Ukrainian and his mother Jewish.

"And how do your identity documents classify you?" I asked. "Are you identified as a Jew or as a Ukrainian?" In the Soviet Union, children of mixed marriages can, on reaching the age of sixteen, choose their nationality. Soviet authorities encourage such youngsters to adopt the nationality of their non-Jewish parent.

"My identity documents," he replied, "classify me as of Ukrainian nationality. But I really don't care. I preferred to be identified as a Jew because of my love for my mother. My father, who has been happily married to my mother for more than twenty years, had no objection. Strangely enough, it was my mother who insisted that I choose the Ukrainian identity. My mother thought that it would help me, as a student, in the advancement of my career if my documents showed that I am of Ukrainian nationality rather than Jewish.

"What my mother does not know yet," he continued, "is that I am soon going to marry a Jewish girl anyway. We are both students in the same class at the university. Nationality means nothing to us. I am sure that neither my mother nor my father will object to our marriage. After all, I am doing the same thing they did. Besides, mixed marriages are a normal development in our country."

Mixed marriages between Jews and non-Jews are a part of the normal way of life among young people in the U.S.S.R. and especially among students. There is practically no prejudice among the student youth.

Contributing greatly to the incidence of intermarriage is the fact that the youth—Jews as well as non-Jews—have no attachment to religion. This does not mean that Jewish youngsters want to divorce themselves from the Jewish identity which is marked in their personal documents. On the contrary, they proudly cling to this identity, although they know nothing about Jewishness. They have no access to knowledge of Jewish history, they are alien to Jewish spiritual achievements, they cannot speak the Yiddish language and do not know a single word of Hebrew, the study of which has been prohibited in the Soviet Union for about fifty years. They read about Israel, but only in the Soviet press, which is anti-Israel.

A young Jew in Russia today knows he is Jewish only because his identity documents are marked with the word "Evrei," which in Russian means "Jew." The great majority of the Soviet-born Jewish youth do not consider this designation an insult. On the contrary, this identification in their passports strengthens their desire to know more about Jews and their past. Some of them find that the word "Evrei" in their documents often stands in the way of their being accepted as students in the university, or of being promoted in employment. Yet the will to know more about Jewishness is strong among them.

On the whole, it can be said that the average young Jew in the Soviet Union feels like an orphan who is eager to find out more about the parents he has never seen. There is very little that his father or mother can tell him about the meaning of

being a Jew, because most of the Jewish parents in the
U.S.S.R. today are either Soviet-born themselves or they were
raised under the Soviet regime. He looks, therefore, to his Jewish grandparents for Jewish guidance—if they are still alive.

Luckily, many Jews in the Soviet Union live a closely knit
family life. This is partly due to the old Jewish tradition in
Russia of having the elder parents live in the same house with
their children and grandchildren. It is also due to the housing
shortage, which forces young adults to live with their parents
and grandparents until they marry and find an apartment for
themselves.

Surviving grandparents, therefore, play an important role in
keeping the younger members of the family Jewish-conscious.
The grandchildren, on the other hand, develop a great affection for the family elders who are their only source of information about Jewish life and traditions. To them, their grand-
fathers and grandmothers are the genuine symbols of
Jewishness and they speak of them with great warmth and admiration. However, this does not prevent the young from entering into mixed marriages.

Soviet authorities publish no data on mixed marriages in the
country. However, such data can be obtained locally in each
city and town, because the marriage offices in each locality
maintain a register showing the nationality of the groom and
the bride.

A look into the marriage register in one of the fifteen city
districts of Moscow establishes that of each one hundred Jewish marriages sixty-six are mixed and thirty-four are nonmixed.
The synagogues in Moscow and in Leningrad maintain special
"marriage chapels" for the use of couples who might want to
satisfy their parents by holding religious marriage ceremonies.
However, the ceremonies performed in these chapels are very
few and their number continues to dwindle with each passing
year, according to synagogue officials.

Mixed marriages are increasing not only among Jews in the
European part of the Soviet Union but also among those in

Central Asia, in such cities as Tashkent and Samarkand. This is true also in distant Siberia and in the remote Ural part of the country, where large industrial centers are being built and where there is a substantial number of Jewish engineers, technicians, and other workers.

In Tashkent alone, which is the capital of Soviet Uzbekistan and has a population of about six hundred thousand, there are today about seventy thousand Jewish inhabitants. The majority of them came there during World War II from the European part of the Soviet Union, from the Baltic states, and from Poland. About one-third of them are reported to be married to non-Jews. They were evacuated in large numbers to Central Asia prior to the entrance of the German armies into the territories where they had lived for generations. After the war was over many of them—but not all—returned to their homes. Polish Jews were given the choice between returning to Poland and remaining in the Soviet Union, automatically losing their Polish citizenship, and becoming a part of the Soviet population.

There was a mass return of Jews to Poland—from where most of them emigrated to Israel—but there were also Polish Jews who for personal reasons chose to remain in the Soviet Union. Some felt that they had adjusted themselves to life in Tashkent, Samarkand, and the other places in Central Asia where they had found work during the war years. Others preferred not to return to Poland because they had in the meantime married Russian women and felt a certain loyalty to the place where they and their non-Jewish wives had lived through the war years. Among the latter were also Jews whose children were born in Asia during the war years and were raised there in schools and by their non-Jewish mothers.

In Moscow I came across a number of Polish Jews who had married non-Jewish girls in Central Asia when they lived there during the war years as refugees whose land was occupied by the Nazis. They now visit Moscow and other cities in the European part of the Soviet Union, but their permanent residence is still in cities in Uzbekistan and Kazakhstan, in Central Asia. Their non-Jewish wives are mostly Russian women who, prior to the entrance of the German Army into their native towns, were evacuated into the Asiatic part of the country, where they found employment in factories and in offices.

These intermarried Polish Jews—who are now Soviet citizens—still live with memories of prewar Jewish life in Poland and are nostalgic for a Jewish atmosphere. Some of them can be found attending synagogue services in the cities where they now reside, the synagogues having been established by them during the early war years when there were among them many religious people who wanted to have a place to worship in. Others among these intermarried Jews express their Jewishness by subscribing to *Sovietish Heimland*, which appears in Moscow once a month.

The nostalgic Jewish feelings of the fathers are, however, completely alien to their children, who do not know Yiddish, since no one in the home speaks Yiddish. The non-Jewish wives love and respect their husbands and do not hide from the children the fact that their father is Jewish. At the same time, both the Jewish father and the non-Jewish mother know that when the children reach the age when they are to choose, under the existing law, whether they want their nationality to be Jewish like the father's or Russian or Ukrainian like the mother's, they will opt for the nationality of their mother. This will remove the last link between them and their origin.

In Siberia and in the Ural region, Jewish assimilation through mixed marriages is proceeding at an even faster tempo. There the Jews are all former residents of the European part of the Soviet Union. There are about forty thousand Jews in Siberia today, in the regions of Omsk, Novo-Sibirsk, and Irkutsk, where the Soviet Government has developed and continues to expand heavy industry enterprises. The Jews there are engaged as skilled workers, engineers, scientists, and laborers. The majority of them are Soviet-born and mixed marriage is to them a normal phenomenon.

The same is true with regard to Jews in the Ural, where according to estimates of Soviet officials there are today about thirty thousand Jews living in newly developed industrial cities. The number of Jewish mixed marriages is very large in cities like Cheliabinsk and Sverdlovsk as well as in several smaller industrial centers. There was a time—in the prewar years —when Jews residing in the European part of the Soviet Union were not keen on moving to the Ural region, although they knew that employment under good conditions awaited them there. They simply did not care to live in this distant section of the country.

Today, young Jewish scientists, engineers, and qualified workers, when meeting with difficulties in securing proper jobs in the central part of the Soviet Union, proceed to the Urals, where they are welcomed and provided with work which promises rapid advancement in view of the constant growth of industrial development in that part of the country, which is rich in natural resources. There is always a shortage of qualified technicians in the Ural industries and feelings of bias against Jews are nonexistent there. On the other hand, the young Jews who choose to live and work there were all born under the Soviet regime; some of them are even second-generation Soviet-born. They adjust themselves in a natural way to the general life there, which is becoming more and more culturally suited to the requirements of a community which is predominantly intellectual.

These young Jews do not think in Jewish terms. To them intermarriage is as normal as any marriage. They marry, and their wives are mostly non-Jewish. The local atmosphere is such that the children don't know whether or not any of their parents are Jewish. Since Jews are given equal opportunity, the "Jewish problem" which exists in other parts of the Soviet Union does not exist there. Complete assimilation is marching fast there. In that section of the Soviet Union there will definitely not be any Jewish continuity.

During my visit in the Soviet Union I came across a few cases of mixed marriages which provoked family problems. These were cases concerning emigration to Israel.

A Jewish man and his non-Jewish wife came to visit me at my hotel. The man is one of those Jewish refugees from Poland who adjusted himself during the war years to Soviet life in Central Asia as a skilled worker. He married his non-Jewish wife there and they now have a son thirteen years of age. Because of his Russian wife the man refused to be repatriated to Poland after the war, preferring to accept Soviet citizenship and remain in Russia.

He had nothing to complain about to me concerning his life in Russia. But he had a brother and two sisters in Israel whom he had not seen since the outbreak of World War II, when they were all young and together. He had corresponded with the members of his family in Israel until the Moscow Government broke off diplomatic relations with the Jewish state. His relatives had suggested that he emigrate to Israel with his wife and boy and they made the necessary formal arrangements.

He confided in me that were it not for his concern over his young son, he would perhaps not be leaving the Soviet Union. His wife, he said, has fears that as a non-Jewess who knows nothing about Jewish life she may feel out of place among Jews in a Jewish country.

"The boy," he said, "is growing up here as a complete non-Jew, totally ignorant of anything that is Jewish. In Israel, I know, he will grow up to be a Jew; here, in the Soviet Union, this will not be the case. He knows that I am Jewish and his mother is Russian; this means nothing to him, just as it means nothing to any Soviet youngster born of a mixed marriage. Not at all religious myself, I would, nevertheless, like my son to know something of Jewish history, Jewish culture, and Jewish life in Israel. I feel that I owe this to him. If he does not like life in Israel he will be able to return to the Soviet Union with my consent. Perhaps my wife and I would then also return. However, I feel I must give my son the chance to get the feel of Jewish life—something he will never get if we remain in the Soviet Union."

His Russian wife, whom I met then for the first time, did not object to their emigration to Israel. "I love my husband and will follow him wherever he goes," she told me. However, she displayed a feeling of uneasiness concerning what might await her boy as the son of a mixed marriage. She had heard that children of mixed marriages are not recognized by the rabbinate to be Jewish children if the mother is not Jewish.

I assured her that her son would, immediately after his arrival in Israel, feel at home in school and on the street and would in no time master the Hebrew language and forget that he had ever lived in the Soviet Union. I have seen this happen to other boys who were brought up in the Soviet Union by Polish-Jewish parents who later emigrated with them to Israel.

I also described to her the life of numerous non-Jewish mothers living in Israel with their husbands and children, and cited examples of several such women who had remained in Israel even after the death of their husbands, although they could have returned with their children to their non-Jewish close relatives in countries like Germany, Poland, and even France.

There was no doubt in my mind that the husband, who had been raised very Jewishly in Poland before he fled to Russia as a victim of the Nazis, was bent on emigrating to Israel, while his wife, who had her roots in Russia—her brother was even a commander in the Red Army—was not enthusiastic about leaving the Soviet Union. This mixed-marriage family was not, however, broken up because of this basic difference in outlook. Mixed marriages are today a very solid family institution in the Soviet Union, since they are built on human relationships and not on religion.

I also came across a similar case that was resolved in the opposite direction. In that case the Jewish husband wanted to go to Israel but his non-Jewish wife did not want to leave the Soviet Union. This time the husband submitted to the wish of his wife.

The wife's resistance to emigration to Israel was not based on ideological factors. Her arguments were primarily economic. Although her husband could, by practicing his profession, make a very comfortable living in Israel for the entire family—himself, his wife, and his school-age daughter— the wife was against moving to Israel because she was a professor of Russian literature in a Soviet University and she did not feel that Israel was a country where she could find a place for herself on a university faculty.

"In Israel," she argued, "they have plenty of scholars of Russian literature. They don't need me there."

The husband had to admit that for a woman like his wife, who had spent many years of specializing in teaching Russian literature before she was given her professorship, Israel had nothing to offer professionally. He accordingly gave up the idea of emigrating to Israel with his family despite the fact that he wanted very much to live in Israel, where he has close relatives who had arranged for his coming to Jerusalem with his family. The sentiments of his non-Jewish wife meant more to him than his personal desire.

Had he insisted on emigration his wife would probably have submitted to his will out of love for him. However, this would have been too much of a sacrifice on her part and he did not want her to bring so great a sacrifice to their mixed marriage. They have been happily married for quite a number of years and he felt that he would have been an unhappy man in Israel if his wife should, on account of his desire to live there, lose the scholarly career and the status which had not been easy for her to reach in the Soviet Union. Certainly his wife would have been an unhappy woman in Israel. And the happiness of his wife, whom he loved and respected, was for him the deciding factor.

♦ ♦ ♦ 12

Young and Old Jews in the Soviet Union

TALKING TO SOVIET JEWS of various ages and professions, one comes to the conclusion that there are four different group reactions inside Soviet Jewry with regard to the treatment of Jewish citizens by the present Soviet regime.

1. *The intellectuals.* These are scientists, physicians, engineers, and other Jews who, because of their advanced and specialized education, hold positions in state institutions, although mostly not the high positions they deserve. They prefer not to discuss the Jewish problem in their country with foreigners. In fact, they prefer not to engage in any talks at all with foreigners.

2. *The elderly Jews.* They still remember vividly the years following the Bolshevik Revolution, when all doors were open to Jews for any government office; when Jewish education flourished in state-maintained Yiddish schools; when the development of Jewish culture was encouraged and even subsidized by the government; when the Jewish religion was combatted like any other religion but synagogues nevertheless functioned in hundreds of cities—each with its own rabbi—and when one could find a kosher restaurant in Moscow, Kiev, Kharkov,

or Minsk. This category of Jews are cautious about expressing complaints to inquiring foreign visitors unless they are certain that no one is eavesdropping on them.

3. *The Jewish youth.* The younger generation of Jews knows nothing of the "better" days for Jews in the early years of the Soviet regime. Most of them were born after World War II, when the "bad years" for Jews started under the aging Stalin, who became strongly anti-Semitic in the last decade of his life. They know they are Jews because their identity documents so state. They don't mind this. What they do mind is the tendency to hold Jews down in their development by making it more difficult for a Jewish youth to enter the school of higher learning or to be advanced in his position to the degree of his ability. They speak openly and without restraint about it even to foreigners. I found them to be the most outspoken and courageous element in Soviet Jewry.

4. *The Jewish Communists.* This is an element which by its very nature constitutes the apologetic group in Soviet Jewry. Jewish members of the Communist Party see nothing wrong with the present status of the Jews in the Soviet Union. They indulge in discussions with foreigners on the treatment of Jews by the Soviet Government in order to promote the government's point of view. They are ready with defensive answers to any question posed to them. Often they leave a foreign visitor with the feeling that their answers are not sincere and that they are merely following the official propaganda line.

It was my first day in Leningrad. I walked into the restaurant at the Astoria Hotel, where I was staying—a very fine hotel very well kept—to have my dinner. The restaurant was brightly lighted, the tables were covered with immaculately clean tablecloths, and people were dancing to the tune of music played by an eight-piece orchestra. I could not believe my ears. The orchestra was playing a Jewish melody which was very popular about fifty years ago among Jews in Poland and in Jewish resort places in the United States.

It was obvious that the members of the orchestra did not suspect that they were playing a Jewish folksong which had been adapted in the Soviet Union to a waltz tempo. Nor did the audience, which enjoyed the tune so much that it asked for it again and again. A vocalist was singing Russian words to the accompaniment of the orchestra and seemed to be enjoying himself no less than the audience. Later I learned that the waltz was known under the name of "Tum Balalaika" and was very popular all over the country.

Small flags of various countries adorned some of the tables, each flag indicating the nationality of the diplomats for whom the table was reserved. Other tables were practically all occupied by Russians in civilian dress, obviously high government officials or well-paid directors of Soviet industrial enterprises who could afford to pay the high price for a meal in this "number-one" restaurant of Leningrad.

The waiter seated me at a small table at which a gray-haired man was already having his dinner. He gave the impression of a highly cultured person, well-dressed, well-mannered, and distinguished looking. He heard me giving my order to the waiter in the Russian language and he apparently assumed that I was a Russian.

"You look very familiar to me," he said in Russian after the waiter disappeared into the kitchen with my order. "I think we met somewhere."

I could see that he was eager to engage in a conversation with me. However, not to cause any embarrassment to him later for speaking to a foreigner, I preferred to identify myself right from the very beginning of the conversation.

"Perhaps you saw me in New York," I said, trying to hint to him that I am an American.

"Oh, you were in New York?" He warmed up to me, not understanding my hint. To him my being permitted to go to New York meant that I was a Soviet citizen fully trusted by the government.

"I live in New York," I finally told him bluntly. "I am an American citizen. I am a journalist who came here from the United States to study the status of the Jews in the Soviet Union."

That was the beginning and the end of our conversation.

The man, who looked Jewish and was probably a scientist, did not utter a single word after I told him who I am. He nervously finished his dinner, paid his bill when the waiter arrived, and very elegantly bowed to me and left the table.

I felt I had spoiled the evening for this polite man. He had come to the restaurant to enjoy a dinner with music and in a relaxing atmosphere, and I had spoiled it for him. Not only did he not want to get into a conversation with me after he learned that I was a foreigner, but he did not want to be seen at the same table with me, even by mere coincidence. He was one of the intellectuals who prefer to be cautious.

I must add that I considered the evening also spoiled for myself. It was my first evening in Leningrad and the incident in the restaurant overshadowed all my thinking the rest of that night.

In Moscow I experienced a less delicate episode, but one also quite expressive of the moods of the "silent men" who prefer not to talk. This time it was with a Jewish scientist who had been banned to Siberia during the period of Stalin's paranoic mistrust of Jews. He was "rehabilitated" immediately after Stalin's death and permitted to return to Moscow, where he was reinstated in his former position. I knew the man many years ago when I was stationed in Moscow as an American newspaper correspondent, and I looked him up now. He was glad to see me and even invited me to have dinner at his house.

I avoided asking him about his painful years in a Siberian prison and I felt that he was grateful for this. Telling me the story of his deportation to Siberia would have meant not only awakening unpleasant memories but possibly also indulging in anti-Soviet expressions—a thing which I sensed he wanted to avoid. For him, his deportation became a closed chapter after his return to Moscow.

I spent a pleasant evening at his home and we talked about all kinds of things, more personal than political. However, when I told him that this time I had come to the Soviet Union for the sole purpose of looking into the treatment of Jews, he had something to say about what he termed "the Jewish problem" in his country. Far from being a Jewish nationalist, he felt that Jews in the Soviet Union would have been better off if their personal documents did not expose them as Jews. He emphasized that he, as a scientist, did not himself suffer on account of the fact that he is identified in his documents as a Jew.

I felt that he was not afraid of my visiting him at his home —otherwise he would not have invited me to dine with his family—but at the same time I also realized that he, too, was among those Jews who preferred to be "silent," especially in talking to a foreigner, even if the foreigner is a good friend. Many such "silent men" among Jewish scientists go as far as absenting themselves from the city rather than to meet even close relatives arriving from abroad to visit them. Some might send their wives to the hotel where the relatives stay in order to see them for a while, but would not invite them to their homes as I was invited by my old friend.

"I hope you are not going to involve me in any way when you write your articles on your visit to the Soviet Union," my friend told me after the dinner was over and he escorted me to the door.

Those were his last words to me when we warmly shook hands at my departure. They said more than anything he told me during the entire evening. He really had told me nothing more than I knew myself and I did not even try to elicit any information from him. I was more interested in him personally than in his views.

I promised him at the door that his name will never be mentioned in any of my articles and I noticed that my promise gave him a feeling of relief. I saw him again before I left Moscow, and this time also in his home. We had a cup of tea and I said good-bye to him and his family. It was a visit of light conversation; no political talk.

In Kiev I came across elderly Jews who were simple people —office workers, bookkeepers, artisans. Most of them had no solid education in Russian but remembered well the Jewish education they had received in their youth. None of them would dare to speak to me on political subjects in their homes, fearing that their neighbors, with whom they shared the same floor, the same kitchen, and the same bathroom, might catch part of their conversation. Individually they were more outspoken—though not fully—when I took a short walk with some of them in the streets, where there is no danger of eavesdropping.

"What would you like me to tell your relatives in New York?" I asked one of them when he escorted me to the bus from his home. I had brought him regards from members of his family in America whom he had not seen for many years but who knew his address and wrote to him without receiving answers.

"Tell them that I am making a living and that my wife and I are in good health. And tell them not to send me letters or parcels." He looked over his shoulder and added: "It is healthier here not to receive mail from abroad."

"I see that you are still living under fear." I felt that I could discuss matters with him more freely on the street than at his home. "You don't even want to hear from your own brother . . ."

He looked over his shoulder again and spoke somewhat apologetically: "You see," he said, "it is very easy for you to talk freely or to ask me pertinent questions. But it is not easy for me to talk to you freely and answer your questions. Certainly I want to hear from my brother. But I know he would not want me to get involved in complications. His letters reach me, but I do not know whether they are opened before delivery, and I do not know whether I am not under suspicion for getting mail from America. Here you have to be careful in such matters. As I told you before, I am making a living and exist like thousands of other Jews here. We are not exactly liked in Kiev, but it is much better living in Kiev than in the provincial towns of the Ukraine, where anti-Jewish bias is felt much more than here."

Another elderly Jew in Kiev summed up the situation for me—also during a walk in the street—by joking about his age.

"You look to me like a man of sixty," I tried to guess.

"But I am only thirty," he replied smilingly.

"Impossible!" I refused to believe him.

"Well," he retorted sarcastically, "if you consider the last thirty years of Jewish life here as living, then I am sixty."

He went on to tell me of the tragic life of the Jews in the years when Stalin encouraged anti-Semitism and when Khrushchev laid the line in the Ukraine of eliminating Jews from conspicuous positions.

"These years left a heavy mark on our life. We Jews in Soviet Ukraine still feel like second-class citizens even today," he added.

The man was more outspoken than other Jews I spoke to. He too said that he was making a living as a qualified worker. He emphasized that he was not religious, but he complained that as a Jew he felt spiritually depressed.

"All Jewish cultural values which I still remember are disappearing fast here," he stated. "Gone are the days when we had a Jewish theater in Kiev, an Institute of Jewish Culture, and other state-supported Jewish cultural institutions. Today the government of Soviet Ukraine does not want to hear about the need for such institutions."

In the Kiev hotel where I was staying—the newly built Hotel Dnipro—I noticed in the lobby a middle-aged Jewish couple watching a group of six American young tourists waiting for a car to take them around town. The group, all men in their twenties, all from Brooklyn, all Orthodox, wore fancy "yarmulkes" (skullcaps), keeping their heads covered in the Orthodox Jewish tradition. They were all American-born but strictly religious. They came on their tour to Russia bringing with them kosher canned foods. They never touched any food in the restaurant of the hotel except bread and tea.

The Soviet Jewish couple were observing them, trying to figure out what nationality they were, without even suspecting that they were Jewish.

"They are probably from Uzbekistan," the woman speculated. "They wear 'tubeteikas' on their heads." (In Soviet Uzbekistan the men do not walk around with bare heads; they wear locally made skullcaps which are known as "tubeteikas.")

"No," her husband disagreed. "They don't look to me like youngsters from Central Asia. I don't understand their language but I think they speak English all the time."

"They are Jewish," I offered my aid to the couple, who conducted their conversation in Russian. "They are young, Orthodox Jews from New York. That is why they keep their heads covered. The skullcap is called a 'yarmulke.' "

Both the man and his wife knew what "yarmulke" meant, but they had never seen a "yarmulke." They had never been to a synagogue where one could still see Jews praying with "yarmulkes" on their heads, although most of them have no "yarmulke" nowadays and use their caps or hats during the prayers instead.

"You mean to say that these young fellows are religious?" The husband looked at me in surprise.

"They are so religious that they brought their own food along with them from America: kosher salami, canned gefilte fish, and other kosher products," I explained to him. "All they eat in the restaurants in the Soviet Union on their tour is fruit, hard-boiled eggs, bread, and tea. They do not even touch cheese or butter."

The Soviet Jewish couple was flabbergasted.

"And are there many Jewish youngsters like these in America?" The husband was curious to know.

"There are Orthodox Jewish schools in New York and in other cities in the United States where children from religious homes get their religious education and continue to observe Jewish religious traditions all their lives," I informed him.

I could read on the man's face that he was impressed. "Do they also speak Yiddish?" he asked.

"Any boy in this group that you see here speaks Yiddish," I told him. "Do you want to speak to them?"

My question provoked uneasiness in both him and his wife.

"No," he said in a tone which denoted fear. "I should not have spoken to you either. You started the conversation with us in Russian and I mistook you for a Russian. Had I known you were a foreigner I would not have discussed these boys with you."

He suddenly felt that he had said too much, so he turned to his wife and told her gently: "I don't think we should wait here any longer. Let's go home!" They had been waiting for a relative who had come from Odessa and was staying at this hotel. But they were afraid to be seen talking to a foreigner in such a public place as the lobby of a hotel.

"Jews live well in America, don't they?" He could not resist implying his impressions about the Orthodox youngsters. "All jobs are open to them, they can travel freely abroad, and they can give their children any kind of Jewish education they want to."

There was a friendly, dreamy look in his eyes as he made this departing remark.

In Moscow and in Leningrad I had opportunities to speak to Jewish young people, both at the universities and in offices. They did not complain of serious anti-Semitism but they emphasized that they came across situations which make them feel that they are not equal citizens.

Like all Jews in the Soviet Union they carry the word "Evrei" on their documents, signifying that they are of Jewish nationality. Eager to know more about their Jewish past and the ancient Jewish culture, they are annoyed by the fact that books on Jewish history are not published in the Soviet Union. Nor have they any access to material on Jewish history which can still be found in special sections of the large libraries in Moscow and Leningrad. They are puzzled as to why the government prevents them from knowing their national history at the same time that all other nationalities in the Soviet Union are proudly studying their ancient past and are developing their national culture without any hindrance.

"We don't want to be ignorant of our Jewish past," a young Jewish officeworker told me in Leningrad in the presence of non-Jewish employees in the same office. "Since I am identified in all my personal documents as a Jew, I may as well know what a Jew is. I know I am not religious; I know of the existence of Israel, but my country is the Soviet Union; I know that the Jewish languages are Yiddish and Hebrew, but

I don't understand either of them—my language is Russian; my Jewishness is attributed to me because of my ancient history, so why should I be prevented from knowing my history?"

It was courageous on the part of this young Jew to speak like this to a foreigner in front of others. Even implied criticism of the government can be considered anti-Soviet propaganda. But I noticed that there was no hesitation on the part of the young man to advance his arguments. What is more— I noticed that the people around him, also youngsters, listened to him with sympathy. Today the young generation of non-Jews in the Soviet Union is also inquisitive. This is especially noticeable in the universities, where the difference between Jews and non-Jews is hardly distinguishable and where Jewish and non-Jewish students think in similar terms.

◆ ◆ ◆ 13

The Jewish Colonies in the Crimea

WHAT HAS BECOME OF the Jewish colonies in the
Crimea which were established by American Jewry through
the Agrojoint—an affiliate of the American Joint Distribu-
tion Committee—in the most difficult prewar years of Jewish life under the Soviet regime? What has happened to the
three hundred thousand Jews who were settled there successfully in the years following 1924 and who became excellent
landworkers over an area of three million acres?

This question has been on my mind since the end of the
war, and long before my recent trip to the Soviet Union. It
was not only a question of general interest for me but also of
personal interest. With Dr. Joseph Rosen, the wonderful per-
sonality and head of the Agrojoint who put so much love and
effort into organizing and carrying out the conversion of "declassed" Jews into admirable farmers, from time to time I visited the colonies as the only American-Jewish journalist stationed in the U.S.S.R. I made a good many personal friends
there among the colonists. What happened to them? What
happened to the farms they built with their own hands in rain
and in wind on land never cultivated before?

What happened to the Jewish post offices in the colonies
where the postage was canceled with official stamps in Yiddish

characters? What happened to the net of Jewish schools and
other institutions which the colonists established? What happened to the colony which carried the name of Sholom Aleichem and to the other settlements in the Crimea named after
Jewish writers? What happened to the settlement of Kalinin-
dorf with its three-room jail which was always empty because
no crimes were committed in the Jewish region?

On my trip to the Soviet Union I hoped to receive permission from the Soviet authorities to revisit the regions where
Jews—former small traders and people without any definite
profession—invested so much of their blood and sweat to
become productive citizens. I knew Hitler's army had ravaged
the Jewish settlements during the Nazi occupation of the Crimea. However, I knew, too, that thousands of Jewish colonists
had succeeded in escaping into the Soviet interior before the
Nazi armies entered their settlements. What happened to these
colonists? Did they return to their homes after the war? Did
they get their land back? Do any signs of Jewish life remain in
the areas where the Jewish colonies were located? If there are
no Jews there now, to whom was their land given after the
war? Who now benefits from the huge efforts which the
Agrojoint made there? Who inherited the property that be-
longed to the Jewish settlers annihilated by the Nazis?

In Moscow, I was told that there was nothing for me to see
in the Crimea now; that the Nazis had killed about ninety
thousand Jews in the Crimea; that of the evacuated Jews, few
returned from the distant places in Central Asia to which they
were transported by the Soviet authorities with some of their
cattle; and that the settlements in the Crimea have been rebuilt
but that they were no longer Jewish. It was indicated to me
that even if I found a Jew here or there, in the settlements, he
would be a member of one of the collective farms now inhabited by Ukrainians.

The Crimea was never a part of the Ukraine. The territory
has a rich history as part of Russia, and not of the Ukraine.
The Turkish-Russian War at the end of the last century was
fought over Crimean ground. During the first years of the Bol-

shevik regime, there were bloody clashes in the Crimea between Czarist military groups and the Red Army which finally ended in the defeat of the Czarist forces. Ukrainians never laid any historic claims to the Crimea. It was therefore puzzling to learn that the Kremlin decided quietly, in 1954, to turn over this rich and strategic Crimea to the Ukrainians and to make it a part of the Soviet Ukraine. Why this was done has never been explained publicly.

Before the outbreak of World War II the Crimea had a large population of Tartars. Although the Jews were settled there after the Soviet Revolution on land which had never been inhabited—where they had to dig wells for fresh water—the Tartars were displeased with the fact that Jews were brought from other parts of the Soviet Union and settled on the land in the Crimea. The Tartars lost nothing by having the Jews as neighbors, since none of their land was taken away for Jewish colonization. On the contrary, they benefited much from the modern methods in farming which Dr. Rosen introduced for the Jewish farmers. In fact, they learned from the Jewish settlers how to work land by tractors—which the Agrojoint brought from the United States—instead of by primitive agricultural methods.

When the Nazi armies started their march on the Crimea, the younger elements among the Jewish settlers were in the Red Army fighting on the front. The Soviet authorities did not want any horses, or cattle, or other inventory to fall into the hands of the Germans. They therefore evacuated many Jewish colonists with their inventory in cattle trains into the far interior of the country. The Tartar population, however, resisted evacuation. When the Nazis later entered the Crimea, they were jubilantly welcomed by the Tartars. The Tartars also saw to it that Jews in hiding were discovered by the Germans and annihilated.

When the Nazi armies were defeated and forced to retreat from the Crimea, Stalin ordered the deportation of the entire Tartar population from Crimea as traitors. Hundreds of thousands of them were deported en masse to remote places in Siberia. They were, however, permitted to return to their homes

after the death of Stalin. But the strategic and rich peninsula
—where the Czar had one of his residences because of the
warm climate—was no longer a Tartar area. Thousands of
Ukrainians were brought over from the Ukrainian towns destroyed by the Nazis during the war and were settled in the
Crimea. The Jewish colonies there became Ukrainian collective farms. Soon the Crimea ceased to be a part of the Russian
Soviet Republic and became an integral part of the Ukrainian
Soviet Republic.

This is the story as presented to me in Moscow in official
circles. In Jewish circles in Moscow I heard an epilogue to
this story throwing light on the mass liquidation of Jewish intellectuals by Stalin. The facts related to me are as follows:

After the German armies retreated from the Crimea, and following the mass deportation of the Tartars for cooperating
with the Nazi occupation forces, leading Jewish Communists
in Moscow, concentrated around the Jewish Anti-Fascist
Committee—the central body of Soviet Jewry which as-
sisted in the fight against the Nazis in the difficult war years
—had an idea. They wanted the restoration of the Crimea as
a Jewish region. They suggested that not only should the survivors of the Jewish colonies be returned to their homes in the
Crimea from the distant parts of the U.S.S.R. to which they
were evacuated, but that all the Jews who had survived Nazi
annihilation in the Ukraine, Byelorussia, and other parts of the
Soviet Union should be brought to the Crimea and resettled
there.

There was plenty of empty land in the Crimea following the
Nazi retreat and the deportation of the Tartars. It was not cultivated and it remained neglected. The leading Jewish Communists felt that after the destruction of Jewish life by the
Nazis in hundreds of towns in the U.S.S.R., the surviving
Jews—even those who had served in the Red Army on the
front—could not return to their former homes because they
were not wanted there by the local non-Jewish population.
What could be more practical, they asked, than to bring all

these Jews to the Crimea and encourage them to start an organized Jewish life there anew?

A memorandum to this effect was submitted by the Jewish
Anti-Fascist Committee to the Kremlin. It was signed by Solomon Mikhoels, the prominent and Soviet-decorated actor who
was the head of the Yiddish State Theater in Moscow, and by
Itzik Feffer, the noted Soviet-Yiddish poet who was promoted
to the rank of Colonel of the Red Army for his services during
the war years. Both were top leaders of the Jewish Anti-Fascist Committee and both of them were the Jews most trusted
by the Kremlin. They had even been sent by the Kremlin to
the United States as a Soviet-Jewish delegation to appeal for
American Jewish aid to Russia in the critical weeks when the
Nazi armies reached Stalingrad.

When the memorandum reached Stalin, no one suspected at
that time that he was paranoic to the extent of planning to
round up all Jews throughout the Soviet Union and isolate
them in Siberia. It was long before the notorious "doctors'
trial," the verdict of which was planned to be a signal for a
wild hunt of anybody whose identity documents were marked
with the word "Jew." When Stalin saw the project outlined in
the Jewish memorandum, he took it as another confirmation of
his suspicion that there existed a conspiracy of "Jewish chau-
vinism" in the country in which even leading Jewish Communists participated. In his perverted mind, he saw in the Jewish
memorandum an effort to strengthen this "Jewish conspiracy."
In his eyes, the Jews in the Soviet Union were not only his
personal enemies but also "the internal enemy" of the country.

The tragic result is well known. Mikhoels and Feffer paid
with their lives. Mikhoels was murdered and Feffer died in a
camp in Siberia. More than two hundred other Jewish
intellectuals—most of them loyal Communists—were "liquidated" by order of Stalin. The Jewish Anti-Fascist Committee was closed. So were all Jewish cultural institutions.

This was the price—I was told in Moscow—Stalin ex-
acted for the suggestion to revive the Jewish colonies and to
normalize Jewish life by settling in the Crimea the Jews left

homeless after the war. Fortunately, Stalin died on March 5, 1953, before the notorious "doctors' trial" was scheduled to open. The trial has never taken place, and the physicians whom he accused of participating in a "Jewish plot" to poison him were released and rehabilitated. Had Stalin lived, deportations of Jews to Siberia would have been started on a large scale, in the opinion today of many Jews in Moscow and Leningrad.

A year after Stalin's death, his successor, Nikita Khrushchev ceded the Crimea to the Ukrainian Soviet Republic. To a delegation of the Canadian Communist Party, Khrushchev declared that he fully agreed with Stalin's policy not to settle Jews in the Crimea because "in case of war, the Crimea can become an anti-Soviet bastion."

Part of the section of the Crimea where the Jewish settlements once existed now seems to be a sensitive area. It has been rumored that the Soviet military authorities established launching stations there from which satellites are being sent into space. These rumors appear to have been proven correct when the American astronaut, Colonel Frank Borman, commander of the Apollo 8 Mission around the moon, made his nine-day visit to the Soviet Union in July of 1969. He was the first foreign airman ever to be taken by the Soviet authorities to the Crimea to observe the launching fields there.

Soviet determination not to resettle any Jews in the Crimea is especially puzzling in the light of the fact that the Jewish colonies which were established there by the Agrojoint contributed very substantially to the advancement of the agricultural system of the entire country. A look in the *Malaya Sovietskaya Encyclopedia*, the 1930 edition, is sufficient to establish that in the whole of the Soviet Union there were only two tractors in the year 1924, when the Agrojoint initiated its activity of transferring declassed Soviet Jews to farmwork in the Crimea and in the Ukraine.

Dr. Rosen, the great American agronomist who went into history as the builder of the settlements for the Jews in the Soviet Union, brought several hundred tractors from the United

States into Russia so that the settlement of Jews on land proceeded in a modern way from the very beginning. While the farmers in the Soviet Union were still tilling their soil with primitive tools, the Jewish colonies started their existence with modern agricultural machinery provided by the Agrojoint, of which James N. Rosenberg, prominent New York attorney, was the chairman.

This revolutionized the entire Soviet agricultural process. Following a policy of encouraging harmony and goodwill between the Jewish settlers and the neighboring groups of other nationalities, the Agrojoint did not restrict its aid to Jews but also promoted the agricultural development of Tartar, Russian, German, and other farms in the area by lending them its Harvester combines, tractors, and other farm machinery, tools, and other implements. The experiments in the modernization of farm work in the Crimea paved the way for the establishment later of collective farms all over the Soviet Union which became the backbone of its entire agricultural system.

In the Agrojoint colonies Dr. Rosen also introduced rotation and diversification of crops by using the proper kinds of seeds. This, too, was recognized by the Soviet Government as an innovation of major importance in Soviet agriculture. It helped to solve Russia's famine problem. Dr. Rosen was also instrumental in reestablishing in Russia, in the Ukraine, a network of pure seed-breeding stations. These were later taken over by the Department of Agriculture of the Soviet Government. American methods of increasing the number of draft animals and dairy cows were also introduced by Dr. Rosen.

Successful from the very beginning in the resettlement of declassed Jews on the land, Dr. Rosen later obtained $8 million from a small group of individuals in the United States interested in helping the Agrojoint work in the Soviet Union. Julius Rosenwald, one of the group, contributed $5 million to this sum. Felix Warburg gave $1 million. The sum of $500,000 was contributed outright by John D. Rockefeller, Jr. This was at a time when American currency meant very much to the Soviet economy, then at its lowest ebb.

The Soviet Government was at that time extremely pleased

with the constructive relief activities of the Agrojoint on behalf of the declassed Jewish population. Some 70 percent of all
the 2,700,000 Jews then living in the Soviet Union had been
deprived of the rights to bread cards, to employment, to
dwellings, and to sending their children to school. They presented quite a problem. They were classified as small traders
who could not be tolerated in a Communist system. The
Agrojoint's coming to their aid by resettling them on land and
also by establishing for them cooperative artisan workshops in
which many were trained to become artisans was, therefore,
welcomed by the Soviet authorities.

Cooperating with the Agrojoint in its effort to settle the
helpless declassed Jews on the land in the Crimea and in the
Ukraine was the Comzet, a body established by the Soviet
Government to help in the Jewish colonization work.
Through the Comzet, free land for Jewish settlement and
tracts of timber to build houses for the settlers were assigned.

The Jewish colonies in the Crimea were established on land
that lay vacant owing to the lack of water. There were six
million acres of such land and the Soviet Government had neither the technical nor the financial means to sink wells there,
although it realized that the success of the Soviet Revolution
depended on increasing the supply of food, which was then ra-
tioned.

The job *was* done, however, successfully by the Agrojoint
with American Jewish funds and American drillers. The desolate, wild, deserted prairies were within one year transformed
into Jewish villages with Jewish farmers who had come to the
steppes without knowing how to handle a plow or to harness a
horse.

Within a few years of their inception, the colonies established by the Agrojoint became the pride of Soviet agricultural
achievement. The Jewish fields in the Crimea, developed under
the guidance of Dr. Rosen, were in a position to compete with
the best fields in Russia. Their wheat was of such quality that
it was used for seeding purposes, and not merely for bread.

In 1938, however, the Soviet authorities liquidated the Agrojoint. By that time the Agrojoint had established 215 settle-

ments, all able to stand on their own feet. More than three hundred thousand Jews were by that time settled on three million acres of land. The Agrojoint had built for them thousands of houses, a number of agricultural schools, and a number of tractor stations.

The parting of the Agrojoint with the Soviet Government was friendly. The Soviet authorities appreciated the tremendous constructive job performed by the Agrojoint but did not want any foreign organization to operate in the U.S.S.R. any longer. It anticipated the forthcoming war and was suspicious of outsiders in the country.

The suspicion of foreigners still exists in the Soviet Union today, long after the war. In the Crimea it was extended also to Tartars and Jews. That the Kremlin still maintains a feeling of suspicion about the Tartars is understandable. They had, after all, cooperated with the Nazi armies during the occupation of the Crimea. But why the feelings of suspicion toward the Jews, who considered the Nazis their mortal enemies? The Jewish colonists were only too eager to be evacuated from the Crimea before the German military entered there.

Otto Ohlendorf, commander of the Nazi extermination units that operated in the Crimea—he was condemned to death by a U.S. military tribunal and executed in 1951—wrote in a report to his superiors in Berlin that the entire area of the Crimea was "Judenrein" (free of Jews) by April 1942. He reported that by that time his units had annihilated approximately ninety thousand Jews who had not been evacuated in time by the Soviet authorities. This left more than two hundred thousand Crimean Jews alive, many of them serving in the Red Army on the battlefronts, and others in the interior of the Soviet Union, where they had been transported when the German armies approached the Crimea.

Many of these two hundred thousand Jews would today welcome the opportunity to return to their old homes in the Jewish colonies in the Crimea and be resettled there on the land on which they had toiled. They would probably be joined also by Jews from other sections of the Soviet Union. However, they are not given this chance. The Soviet Govern-

ment does not want the Jews to take root now in the Crimea
—where the historic Yalta agreement was signed by Stalin,
Roosevelt, and Churchill. It considers the peninsula of strategic
importance and, as Khrushchev indicated, does not want any
concentration of Jews there.

••• 14

At Babi Yar in Kiev

YOM KIPPUR, the Day of Atonement, is the most
sacred day of the year for Jews everywhere. For Jews in Kiev,
the capital of Soviet Ukraine, the two days preceding Yom
Kippur are the most sacred.

They are "The Babi Yar Days."

Two days before Yom Kippur in 1941—on September 29
and 30—the German Army, having occupied the city only
ten days earlier, drove the Jews to the Babi Yar ravine at the
outskirts of the city and mowed them down. The massacre
ended on Yom Kippur eve, when Jews throughout the world
prayed "Kol Nidrei" in the synagogues.

An official Nazi report of the massacre sent to Colonel Rein-
hard Heydrich, the deputy chief of the Gestapo, said that
33,771 Jews were executed at the ravine during the two days
of mass killing, but the number was much larger. Later, about
fifteen thousand more Jews were killed.

The Germans entered Kiev on September 19, three days before Rosh Hashonah, the Jewish New Year. A few days after
their arrival a tremendous explosion rocked the Continental
Hotel where the German military command made its headquarters. The explosion was caused by powerful time bombs
placed by the Red Army prior to its retreat from the city. It

touched off hidden land mines in the area and set many buildings afire. So sweeping was the blaze that hundreds of German soldiers were killed while fighting it.

The German occupation authorities decided to blame the Jews for this catastrophe. On September 26, three days after Rosh Hashonah and five days before Yom Kippur, notices were posted all over Kiev ordering all Jews of the city to assemble with all members of their families, at eight o'clock in the morning on September 29 at the corner of Melnikov and Degtyrov streets, near the cemetery. The notices said that the Jews were earmarked for "resettlement." They "advised" each Jewish family to take along a bundle containing its valuables, warm clothing and underwear, and food for several days.

The notices emphasized that those who did not appear at the given time and place would be shot when discovered later. Tens of thousands of Jews trekked with their bundles from all parts of the city and appeared early in the morning, many of the women carrying children in their arms. Most of the men were elderly and sick since the able bodied were already mobilized into the Red Army.

The streets around the gathering place were surrounded by units from the "Einsatzgruppen"—the Nazi murder commandos who specialized in mass killing of Jews. The arriving Jews were marched in groups, past the Jewish cemetery at the outer city limits, to the Babi Yar site; they were ordered to leave their bundles and were later driven naked into the ravine.

During the two days of the terror, the shooting of the victims went on from dawn till dark. It was later reported that the Nazis who did the shooting cared nothing whether some of their victims were still alive in the ravine. One group after the other was driven into the ravine while some of the people who were shot still showed some signs of life. They were directed to lie down on top of the bodies that lay before them and were machine-gunned in cold blood. In the evening the Germans stopped the shooting, herding the still living Jews into empty stables for the night, resuming the extermination the next morning.

The murder rate of the two-day massacre exceeded even that of the mass killings of Jews in the gas ovens of the most notorious Nazi death camps of Auschwitz and Treblinka in Poland. Five months after the executions, the March thaw released gases from thousands of bodies in the ravine with explosions which threw up columns of the earth covering the victims.

In the days between Rosh Hashonah and Yom Kippur today, thousands of Jews in Kiev stream to Babi Yar every year to lay flowers in memory of their fathers, mothers, wives, and children who were so brutally killed. The majority of those paying their annual commemoration visit to the mass grave of their nearest and dearest are men. They were in the Red Army ranks of the war front fighting the German invaders when Kiev was occupied by the Hitlerites. Some of them were, as qualified workers, evacuated from Kiev with the factories where they worked prior to the occupation.

They returned home after the liberation of Kiev but found none of the members of their families alive. The Babi Yar tragedy will remain with them for the rest of their lives. They observe the "anniversary" of the massacre by coming to Babi Yar from all parts of the city. They are joined by thousands of Jews who settled in Kiev after the war and whose families were similarly killed in pits on the fringes of cities where they resided.

Babi Yar is also visited by Jews from foreign countries who come to Kiev as tourists. In fact, one of the main reasons that most of these tourists visit Kiev is to pay their respects to the dead at Babi Yar. However, the local Intourist office discourages foreigners from visiting Babi Yar. Soviet authorities, central and local, are not eager to present the massacre as a Jewish tragedy. To get to Babi Yar without the aid of Intourist is not an easy matter and not all private taxis know the road.

In the Hotel Dnipro—the finest hotel in the city, which was built after the liberation of Kiev—I consulted the information desk of Intourist, which is supposed to help foreign visitors with information about how to get to Babi Yar. The girl in charge of the desk was evasive. When I insisted on getting the information, she said she herself did not know how to get to Babi Yar and would have to inquire from others in the office. She suggested that I come back in about one hour.

"You mean to say that you, a resident of Kiev, don't know where Babi Yar is located?" I was astonished.

The girl was embarrassed. She saw I didn't believe her.

"A lot of people in Kiev do not know where Babi Yar is," she replied. "It is somewhere on the outskirts of the city."

"But you certainly know that one of your great poets, Yevgeni Yevtushenko, has immortalized the place with the famous epic poem 'Babi Yar' which was translated into many languages throughout the world?"

She knew about Yevtushenko's poem. And so do all the young people in Kiev. Despite the fact that Yevtushenko was criticized by Soviet authorities for writing this poem honoring the memory of the Jews who perished. Yevtushenko, a Ukrainian writer in the Russian language, is the most popular Soviet poet among the student youth in all of the Soviet Union. His poem is considered a memorial to the Jewish victims of Babi Yar. After it was published Intourist could no longer tell foreign visitors that nobody knew anything about Babi Yar, as officials of Intourist claimed before the poem appeared.

The Intourist girl repeated her request that I return in about an hour if I wanted to get information about how to get to Babi Yar, and it became obvious to me that she was obliged to report my request to some higher officers. I was resigned to her request, and told her that I would be back in about an hour. But at this point something quite unexpected happened. A young man who was watching me in the lobby arguing with the girl approached me in very fluent English after I left the desk.

"You want to go to Babi Yar? Come, I'll take you. I know where the place is. You will not have to pay me anything. All you will have to pay is the fare to the taxi driver."

I was taken aback by this sudden offer. "Are you an Intourist guide?"

"No," he replied smilingly. "I am a university student. I overheard your discussion with the Intourist girl and I decided that you needed my help. The girl was trying to discourage you from visiting Babi Yar and will probably find a new excuse to discourage you. But I want to encourage you. I have a personal interest in doing it. Some of my relatives were massacred in Babi Yar and I think that this massacre should not be forgotten. There should be no 'hush-hush' about it. The more people who see Babi Yar, the longer the world will remember the Nazi atrocities."

"But you don't look Jewish to me," I said and implied that I was surprised by his offer.

"I am half-Jewish," he said with a wide smile. "And it makes no difference to me, or to my parents, whether I am Jewish or not. I am by my upbringing and nationality a Ukrainian. But my mother is Jewish. She was not in Kiev when the Germans killed the Jews. Nor was I. I wasn't even born then. But we know about everything that took place at Babi Yar, and so does almost every student in the university. Yevtushenko's poem has greatly contributed to it. After his poem appeared, a number of other students and I visited Babi Yar several times. That is how I know the place. You will not see anything there now but you have to visit this place anyway. Everybody who comes to Kiev has to visit Babi Yar."

The taxi driver whom I hired to take us to Babi Yar told me in advance that he did not know where the place was located or how to get there. However the student told him not to worry. He directed him all the way until we reached the assembly site. Here he told the driver to stop. The taxi halted and my young volunteer guide explained: "Here, at this place, the Jews from all parts of the city were ordered to appear with food for three days. They were told that they would be sent from here to work and would be resettled in new places. The Jews believed it. They assembled here on time, as ordered. From here they were marched in groups to their death to Babi Yar."

He went into details of the event, and I could see that the taxi driver, a non-Jew, was as deeply interested as I in what the young student related. The driver probably never heard

these details before, since the Soviet press never reported the
Babi Yar case in details. We climbed back into the taxi and the
driver showed a special eagerness to reach Babi Yar.

"You will not see much at the place now," the student, no-
ticing his sudden interest, told him in Ukrainian. "The place
has changed. Nobody who remembers Babi Yar from the year
of the great massacre will recognize it now."

The place had changed. You come to the ravine where tens
of thousands of bodies of the killed Jews were barely covered
with earth, and what do you see there now? No sign of a ravine. Now apartment buildings stand on the place where the
massacre took place. None of the dwellers even thinks of the
fact that the building where he resides has been built on heaps
of bones of human beings.

A wooded area has been developed over the ravine with
rows and rows of young trees planted to cover the ground
which was soaked with the blood of so many thousands. Instead of erecting a huge granite memorial tomb and make the
place a shrine, the Soviet authorities chose to cover up one of
the greatest of the Nazi war crimes by converting Babi Yar
into a development area and giving it an appearance of seren-
ity and innocence.

A small square near the wooded section was left untouched
by the authorities. Here a small primitive gray stone stands in
the center as a reminder of the 1941 tragedy. One can hardly
read the inscription on the epitaph dedicated to the victims
buried beneath it. And even this description does not mention
the truth about the tragedy—that the victims were primarily
Jews.

"The authorities have promised to erect an impressive monument here and have even reported that there will be a worldwide competition in which sculptors will submit projects for
such a monument. However, nothing has been heard of any
further action with regard to the monument," the student told
me and the driver in a painful tone. "The entire matter seems
to be a forgotten thing."

Whether a decent monument will ever be erected on the

Babi Yar grounds or not, it is clear that neither the Soviet authorities in the Ukraine nor the central government in Moscow have any interest in commemorating the tens of thousands of massacred Jews even though they were killed by the Germans.

The Jews residing now in Kiev still deeply mourn the Babi Yar dead every year in the week between Rosh Hashonah and Yom Kippur during the days which Judaism calls "The Days of Awe" but which the Kiev Jews call "The Babi Yar Days." Every year they come with flowers on these days and place them in front of the small stone which the Kiev Soviet has put up on the small square of land not yet covered by new apartment buildings or woods. They all come, their heads covered, and those among them who can still recite a Jewish prayer do so; others just shed a tear.

The autumn wind was blowing very hard when I visited Babi Yar. It tore the leaves from the bundles of flowers placed at the marking stone and carried them away in the direction of the buildings erected on the ravine. Tomorrow there would be rain and mud—no day for laying flowers. Yet there would be Jews whom neither the rain nor the mud, nor the deep snow later, would deter from visiting Babi Yar. The Jewish mass grave may be covered up with young trees and new apartment buildings, but Kiev Jews will never forget the Babi Yar tragedy. Nor will Jews throughout the world. And who knows? Just as the Jews in all the free countries of the world now recite each year a special prayer at the Passover Seder for the martyrs of the Warsaw Ghetto, they may also compose and recite a special prayer on Yom Kippur for the martyrs of Babi Yar.

This would perhaps be the best monument Jews can erect for the thousands and thousands of Jews killed in the unforgettable ravine and in the ravines of other cities in the Soviet Union.

The Simchas Torah Mass Demonstrations

To BE IN MOSCOW and not to witness the huge Jewish mass demonstration on the Jewish holiday of Simchas Torah—which usually falls in October—is like being in New York on New Year's Eve and not seeing the huge crowd out on Times Square to meet the new year.

Simchas Torah is the holiday when the annual reading of the Torah is finished in the synagogue and is commenced anew for the starting new year. It is a joyous holiday. The mass demonstration in Moscow marking it attracts between twelve thousand and fifteen thousand Jews from all parts of the city. The demonstration takes place on Archipova Street —about ten minutes' walk from the Kremlin—in front of Moscow's Central Synagogue.

This demonstration is significant firstly because it is the only huge non-Communist street mass rally tolerated by the Soviet authorities. Secondly, because the demonstration takes place against a religious background. Thirdly, because most of the participants in the demonstration are young people— primarily students. A similar demonstration, on a smaller scale, also takes place on the same evening in Leningrad in front of the magnificent Choral Synagogue there. But no such demonstrations are permitted in cities like Kiev, Odessa, and other centers with a large Jewish population, and certainly not in the smaller cities.

Foreign diplomats in Moscow assume that the Simchas Torah demonstrations in Moscow and in Leningrad are tolerated by the Soviet authorities because in these two cities there are many foreign observers—diplomats, correspondents, and tourists. The theory is that the authorities cannot suppress the Jewish mass demonstrations in these two cities because any police action against the demonstrators would have strong reverberations abroad. It would also serve as proof that religion is being suppressed in the Soviet Union, whereas the Soviet Government maintains that the state does not interfere in religious affairs. Foreign embassies usually watch the Simchas Torah demonstrations in Moscow and Leningrad very closely as do all the foreign correspondents.

The Soviet authorities in Moscow are discounting these demonstrations as a mere show of desire on the part of the Jewish youth "to have a good time." They consider them to be neither of political nor of religious importance. There are no political speeches delivered at the demonstrations. The merry street dancing which lasts all evening and into the after-midnight hours is marked by the singing of Jewish melodies and by the lighting of newspapers as primitive torches which add a festive atmosphere to the night dancing under the open sky.

"Would you call this a religious festival?" an important Soviet official argued with me the day after Simchas Torah. "You saw the young people yourself; would you say that they have any religious sentiments? Many among them are not even Jews, according to our information. They simply join the crowd to dance. I can tell you that among the dancing youngsters there is quite a number of members of the Comsomol, the organization of young Communists. They come to dance without being aware, even, of the fact that they are helping to celebrate a Jewish religious holiday."

It is probably true that there are many young Communists

among the participants in the demonstration. However, in personal talks with many of the young people in the crowd—boys and girls alike—I established that they all know what the festival is about. They know nothing about the Jewish religion, but are aware of the meaning of Simchas Torah as a Jewish religious holiday dealing with the Torah. Hundreds of them are not satisfied with merely dancing in the street. They push to get inside the overcrowded synagogue just to be able to kiss the Torah there or at least to observe others kissing the Torah during the "Hakofot"—the seven processions in which Jews with the Scroll of Law in their arms parade it inside the walls of the synagogue.

As to the political character of the mass demonstration, the authorities see to it that even any slight attempt on the part of anybody in the crowd to give a political twist to the festival —through speeches or slogans—is immediately suppressed. Mingling with the crowd are uniformed policemen and political secret-service agents.

In the year 1967—the year when Israel won the Six Day War with the Arabs and when the Soviet Government, backing the Arabs, broke diplomatic relations with the Jewish state—a few young men at the Simchas Torah street demonstration in front of the Leningrad Synagogue started to shout "Long Live Israel!" They were immediately arrested on the spot and were later put on trial.

The next year the Soviet authorities did not prohibit the Simchas Torah demonstration. However, they restricted the demonstration to the synagogue yard. The crowd was not permitted to extend to the street. Huge bulldozers were placed on the street, facing the synagogue, so that no space was left for crowds to gather.

The Leningrad Jewish youth took the hint. Instead of the usual ten thousand youngsters that participated the year before in the Simchas Torah celebration, only about four thousand showed up in 1968. The rest were afraid even to be seen near the synagogue after the arrests of some of their friends in 1967. The majority of them being students, they did not want to risk expulsion from the university just for being seen by secret

BAKING OF MATZO for Passover was prohibited in the Soviet Union after 1962. Under protests from Jews in the United States and other free countries, the ban was somewhat relaxed for Jews in Moscow. Not until 1969 was the baking of matzo permitted for Jews in all parts of the Soviet Union.

BABI YAR. Thirty years after the mass execution by the Nazis of tens of thousands of Kiev Jews, in September 1941, at the Babi Yar ravine; the Soviet Government has still not permitted any monument to be erected for the Jewish victims. The local Soviet authorities have put up some apartment buildings in a section of the area, but the place still looks neglected and desolate. An epic poem, "Babi Yar," dedicated to the Jewish victims was written by the famous Soviet poet Yevtushenko. He was criticized for doing it. The poem has been published in many countries and translated into many languages.

JEWISH CEMETERY IN MINSK, destroyed and desecrated. Minsk is the capital of Soviet Byelorussia and was one of the large Jewish centers. It is estimated that there are today 135,000 Jews in Byelorussia. In most of the cities there are no synagogues functioning. In Minsk, the local authorities dissolved the prayer groups in private Jewish homes and confiscated their Torah Scrolls.

MEMORIAL TO JEWISH VICTIMS IN VILNA. While Soviet authorities do not permit the erection of monuments on the graves of the mass-murdered Jews by the Nazis in other Soviet cities, such a monument was permitted by the Soviet Lithuanian government in the city of Vilna. The inscription is in Yiddish and in Russian.

ROSH HASHONAH SERVICES IN RIGA SYNAGOGUE. The Jewish New Year of 5728 (1968) is observed with prayers in the Riga synagogue, with the women separated on the balcony in accordance with the Jewish Orthodox tradition. It is noted that few of the praying men are in the traditional prayer shawls and none in the traditional scull-cap known as yarmulke. This indicates the lack of traditional Jewish garb among the faithful in the Soviet Union.

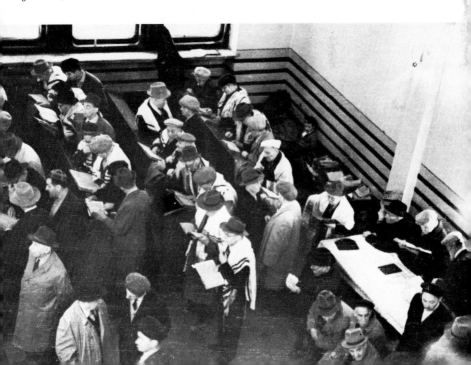

JEWISH FUNERAL IN MOSCOW. The scene of a Jewish funeral service in a Moscow suburban synagogue.

THE SYNAGOGUE IN ODESSA before it was set afire and after the fire. *(on facing page)*

POLICE BARRIERS AT LENINGRAD SYNAGOGUE. The photo shows the barriers erected by the police in the yard of the Leningrad synagogue on the eve of Simchas Torah in 1969 to prevent mass celebration of the holiday on the street by thousands of Jewish youngsters, mostly students.

SYNAGOGUE IN MOSCOW. (Photo by Dr. Abraham I. Katsh.)

ISRAELIS GREETED BY JEWS IN MOSCOW. Moscow Jews meeting a group of young Israelis who came to take part in the Youth Festival in Moscow (July-August 1957). This was ten years before the Soviet Government broke off diplomatic relations with Israel and put itself fully on the side of the Arabs in the Arab-Israeli War. Notice the Soviet uniformed police. (Photo by YIVO Institute for Jewish Research.)

IN FRONT OF MOSCOW SYNAGOGUE. Jews gather in front of Moscow's Great Synagogue on the eve of a Jewish holiday, in 1966.

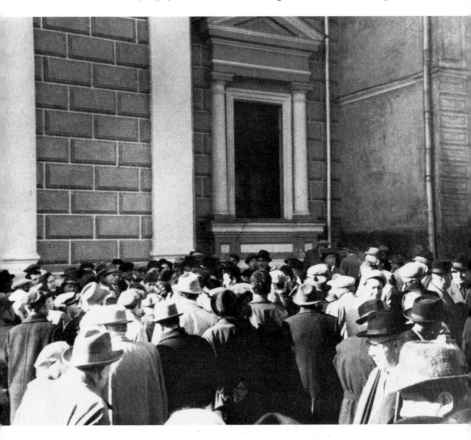

INSIDE THE KIEV SYNAGOGUE. A group of elderly Jews inside the synagogue in Kiev. (Photo by Dr. Abraham I. Katsh.)

JEWS PRAYING IN LENINGRAD SYNAGOGUE. Leningrad Jews at prayer in the Choral Synagogue on Rosh Hashonah, the Jewish New Year. (Photo by Dr. Abraham I. Katsh.)

PRAYER FOR PEACE, huge tablet in Russian and in Hebrew erected in the synagogue of Marina-Roshtsha, a Moscow suburb. The tablet is placed side by side with the Holy Ark where the Torahs are kept, in the most honored spot in the synagogue.

JEWISH YOUTH PROTEST IN NEW YORK. An open-air protest meeting of Jewish youths in New York, under the slogan "Let My People Go," demands the permission by the Soviet Government of emigration of Jews to Israel and the release of a number of Jews arrested by Soviet authorities for seeking such emigration. The names of some of the arrested are indicated in the placards carried by the demonstrators. (Photo by Itzhak Berez.)

agents in the crowd near the synagogue. There are not a few students who as active Communists perform the role of agents for the political secret service. To be recognized by them at the Simchas Torah demonstration and denounced is something which very few Jewish students in Leningrad could afford. In 1969 the police closed the street where the synagogue stands and dispersed the several thousand youths who dared to gather outside of that building.

Leaders of the Leningrad Synagogue told me that in their opinion it was quite "foolish" on the part of the few youngsters to shout at the Simchas Torah rally such slogans as "Long Live Israel!" and thereby jeopardize the event which is the only expression of Jewishness among the assimilated Jewish youth of the city. No such moves have been made in Moscow during the Simchas Torah demonstration. When I witnessed the Moscow demonstration in 1968 the crowd was orderly and the police were polite. Israeli songs were sung by the demonstrators but without words. Just the melodies. And this was the case also inside the overcrowded synagogue where all evening the audience sang many popular Israeli tunes, but without their texts. Singing the words could have been interpreted by the Soviet authorities as being publicly pro-Israel at a time when the Soviet Government brands Israel as an enemy and when the Soviet press and radio blast Israel daily since the 1967 June war, without a letdown.

The Simchas Torah demonstrations in Moscow and Leningrad are a comparatively new phenomenon. They started several years ago spontaneously, without being organized by anyone. They began to draw larger and larger crowds with every year. They are not advertised or announced in advance, but somehow thousands of Jewish youths make it their business to find out on what day Simchas Torah occurs and in the evening they appear in mass in front of the synagogues to celebrate the holiday.

The celebration usually starts at seven o'clock in the evening. When I arrived at six o'clock, the entire Archipova Street was already overcrowded with people, from one end of the street to the other. It was impossible to make a move once you were in the crowd. You could neither push yourself forward nor make your way backward. You were carried by the crowd, which was drifting toward the center of the street to be right in front of the synagogue entrance.

Police units were engaged on the corners of Archipova Street in redirecting the traffic. Some of them were busy maintaining order politely among the growing crowds on the side streets, who had come too late to penetrate into Archipova Street. A large number of police cars and ambulances were lined up on the side streets in reserve, ready for emergency action.

It did not take me long to realize that I would never succeed in pushing myself into Archipova Street. I therefore decided on direct action. I approached the police captain whom I had observed giving instructions to police details at the corner of Archipova and Khmelnitzky streets. Addressing him in Russian, I said: "I am an American Jew now visiting your country. I would like to attend tonight's holiday in the synagogue. Could you be of help to me in reaching the entrance into the synagogue through this crowd?"

The police captain smiled politely and his first remark was: "I congratulate you on your holiday!" ("S Prazdnikom!")

I must admit that I was taken aback by this greeting coming quite unexpectedly from a higher police official. It sounded very natural and sincere. Shrugging his shoulders as indication of sympathy with my request, which seemed to him impossible to fulfill, he continued with utmost politeness: "See for yourself!" he said. "You cannot drop a pin into this huge and tight crowd. How could I undertake to bring you to the synagogue, when nobody can move even a few steps from here in this mass of people!" . . .

He stood for awhile as if giving a second thought to my request, and then said: "Let me try! . . . I have policemen stationed within the crowd . . . A detail of two policemen every two hundred steps . . . They are there to prevent disorder . . . I will assign one of my policemen here to make way for you through the crowd till you reach our first two policemen inside the crowd. My man will carry a verbal order from me to one of the two policemen to leave his post and bring you to the next detail and then return immediately to his post. At the next detail, one policeman will leave his post to take you to the next unit of two policemen stationed further in the crowd and then also return immediately to his post. And so my men will make way for you through the crowd from post to post until you reach the entrance to the synagogue.

"However," he added smilingly, "don't expect a policeman to bring you further than the entrance. At the entrance you will have to find your own way into the synagogue. Our police have strict instructions not to enter the synagogue and not to disturb the service."

I thanked him profusely for his special effort. He called over a policeman from his detail and gave him the necessary instructions, emphasizing that he could speak to me in Russian in case of any complication. The policeman had no great difficulty in pushing his way through the mass ocean of people with me following him. He brought me to the first two policemen stationed within the crowd, and returned to his captain. A policeman then made way for me to the next station, and a policeman from the next station took me through the crowd to a further station, until I reached the front of the synagogue.

To enter inside the synagogue one must climb several steps. However, I was spared this effort. I did not enter the synagogue; I was carried into it by the waves of people pushing from the street to the doors of the building. In fact, I did not feel any ground under my feet when carried by the crowd into the synagogue. I was impelled inside the synagogue by a throng of people who were themselves crowded by others, and suddenly found myself in the midst of a Simchas Torah service the like of which one cannot see anywhere in the Jewish world.

It was now pouring outside, but the crowd on Archipova Street continued to grow. The rain did not prevent the growing crowd from singing and feeling happy. Few had come with umbrellas, but it would even have been impossible to open an umbrella in the tight crowd.

Inside the synagogue, the congestion was no less than on the street. There were probably more than two thousand people, young and old, crowding the benches, the passages, the galleries, and every nook and corner. There was a holiday spirit in the air. Young men who noticed that they were bareheaded felt a kind of guilt for not having their heads covered in this holy place. They automatically used their handkerchiefs as temporary cover. Young girls similarly sought to keep their heads covered, adding solemnity to the atmosphere.

It was obvious that the young people in the overcrowded synagogue were not religious, but it was also obvious that they had not come for the sake of curiosity. It is the strong desire for Jewish identity which brought them, identity of which they are aware only because their personal documents mark them as Jews.

Unlike in the United States, where the Jewish religious community is divided into three denominations—Orthodox, Conservative, and Reform—Jews in Russia have never practiced anything but the Orthodox form of religion. This is the case with religious Jews in the Soviet Union even today. Other forms of Jewish religion are completely alien to them. On Simchas Torah you see the Jews in the Central Moscow Synagogue celebrating the holiday in the traditional Orthodox way and with the kind of joy one sees only in the extreme Orthodox prayerhouses in New York.

Up on the pulpit, near the Ark of the Holy Scrolls, the aged rabbi, Yehuda Leib Levin, was standing, surrounded by the gray-bearded president of the synagogue and other synagogue dignitaries. He chanted the Simchas Torah evening prayers to an ancient melodious tune, provoking nostalgic inspiration among the elderly religious Jews and awesome respect among the younger people who had never learned to read the prayers. The compact audience grew even tighter as the moment approached for opening the Holy Ark to take out from there the Scrolls for the Hakofot processions within the synagogue.

The moment arrived. With thousands of eyes directed toward the pulpit, eager not to miss a single moment of what was taking place, the massive audience saw the president of the synagogue take out one Torah after another—about ten altogether—and hand over the first Torah to the rabbi as leader of the procession. Calling out the names of the other dignitaries honored to be among the first to carry a Torah in the first procession, the president handed a Holy Scroll to each of them and the chanting procession from the pulpit started into the crowd.

"How will they push themselves through with the Scrolls in this mass of people which is so knitted together?" I was wondering.

The answer came by itself. Somehow in all this tightness space was miraculously made by the onlookers to let the procession pass and make its round back to the pulpit. Young and old standing on both sides of the passage struggled to get close to the bearers of the Torah in order to be able to kiss the Holy Scroll, or at least to reach the Torah with their fingers and caress it. It was most remarkable to see the enthusiasm with which the adolescent boys and girls kissed the Torah, the contents of which they had never been permitted to study under the Soviet rule.

The dignitaries completed their round of the procession and found themselves back, with the Torahs in their arms, at the pulpit, from which the procession had begun. Now a second procession started with the same Torahs. This time the oldest members of the synagogue were the Torah bearers making the circle. Again youngsters rushed toward them, seeking a chance to be able to kiss the Scroll or at least to touch it gently.

The third procession was about to start, and here something unexpected happened. The president announced from the pulpit: "This procession is intended only for people under thirty years of age!". . .

The youngsters in the audience, taken by surprise, were jubilant. It was obvious that the decision to hand over the third procession to the younger people had as its aim to make them feel that they are considered part and parcel of the Jewish community although they had no religious upbringing. The announcement was to them like a bombshell. Each of the young men in the synagogue was now propelling himself forcefully to the pulpit to be among the fortunates who would be included in the procession.

Few, however, succeeded in moving from the places where they were stranded. Only those closest to the pulpit were lucky enough to be among the ten to whom the Torah Scrolls were handed over at the pulpit to make the third round. Their faces shining with happiness, the ten youths followed the path which the previous two processions had taken, moving slowly, with the Torahs in their arms under the siege of other young people—boys and girls—who now felt more courageous in seeking to get closer to the Scrolls, since the bearers were of their own age.

The young Torah bearers, feeling the strong desire on the part of their young friends and colleagues to also share in the carrying of the Holy Scrolls, each stopped during the procession and handed over their Scroll to other youngsters, and the latter followed this example by handing over the Scroll several minutes later to other young people who could never have reached the pulpit because they were too far from it. The ten Torahs thus changed many hands during the procession, making many youngsters happy.

The remaining four processions were mixed—with old and young people bearing the Scrolls, and each of the two groups feeling happy. The elderly Jews felt happy over the fact that not all the Soviet Jewish youngsters were lost to religion, and the young participants felt happy that they were among the few fortunates who were given the privilege of carrying the Holy Scroll on Simchas Torah.

It was obvious that these young people will remember their experience this evening for the rest of their lives.

Two questions interested me while watching the fervor of the thousands of Jewish youngsters who had come from all parts of Moscow to participate in the mass celebration at the synagogue although they knew nothing about Judaism and the holiday.

One question was: How did so many young Jews in Moscow—who are strangers to the Jewish religion—find out that tonight is Simchas Torah?

The second question was: What brings them to the celebration when they are actually not religious?

I posed these questions to dozens of youngsters in the crowd. The answers were various.

"How did we find out that tonight is Simchas Torah?" a young girl replied, looking mischievously at other youngsters around her. "Well, we heard it announced over the radio . . . !"

"Over the radio?" I was puzzled. "You mean to say that the Moscow Radio reported that Simchas Torah would be celebrated at the synagogue here tonight?"

The girl laughed a hearty and carefree laugh. "Who told you that we heard it on the Moscow Radio?" she said. "There are also other radio stations."

The other youngsters around her smiled. They seemed to like her daring answer. What she implied was that the youth listens clandestinely to forbidden broadcasts from foreign stations. The American radio station in West Germany makes it a part of its program to broadcast announcements of forthcoming Jewish holidays. So does the Israeli radio station from Tel Aviv. So does the British Broadcasting Corporation from its station in London. All these broadcasts are beamed to Russia, and some of them are given in the Russian language. On Rosh Hashonah, on Yom Kippur, on Passover, they even carry part of the Jewish services in the hope that Jews in Russia will listen in and will not forget their holidays.

A young man in another group was even more outspoken in his answer to my question as to how he discovered that tonight is Simchas Torah. Looking at the others around him and sensing their approval, he let himself go quite unreservedly.

"We students," he said, "have no difficulty finding out when the Simchas Torah celebration takes place. You come in the morning to the university, and on the bulletin board there you see a brief announcement put up by some anonymous hand. It reads: 'Sevodnia Vecherinka!' ('Tonight we have a good time!') Many Jewish students know that this actually means: Tonight is the mass celebration of Simchas Torah in front of the synagogue! They tell it to others who don't know the meaning of the innocent two-word message on the bulletin board. The signal, as you can see here, serves effectively. It brings student crowds and their friends to the front of the synagogue even before the evening starts."

Other young people in the crowd revealed to me other ways they find out when Simchas Torah is being celebrated.

"My grandmother is my Jewish calendar," a girl in the crowd explains. "My grandmother knows all the Jewish holidays and tells me about them. She lives with us and I love her dearly. She told me this morning that tonight is Simchas Torah, so I conveyed the information to a number of my girl friends and we all came here. I know my grandmother herself would have been here if she were not so aged. She is glad that I am here, and so am I. It makes me feel so much closer to my family!"

A young man tells me that he solves his Simchas Torah problem in a very simple way. In the early days of October he telephones the office of the synagogue for information, and gets the exact date on which Simchas Torah falls that year. So far he has never failed to attend the Simchas Torah mass demonstration.

To the question as to what brings them to the celebration although they are not religious, I received practically the same answer from all. The answer was: "We came here because we are Jews." The fact that Simchas Torah is a religious holiday does not matter to them.

"I know nothing about my being Jewish except that my identity document marks me as such," a young man in the crowd told me. "But once I am a Jew, I want to belong to the Jewish people—a kind of pride of nationality. Participating in the Simchas Torah mass celebration gives me this feeling of belonging. It has nothing to do with religion. To me Simchas

Torah is not a religious holiday, but a holiday that reflects optimism and joy. At the celebration we, the younger people, express our belonging to Jewry, not through prayers but through singing and street dancing and merriment."

The same sentiments were expressed to me by most of the other young people. The merry spirit of Simchas Torah is what attracts them and the fact that they can give expression to their Jewish feelings in an atmosphere of singing Jewish melodies and dancing to Jewish tunes. I tried to find out why they don't come to the synagogue on Rosh Hashonah and Yom Kippur and the answer was: "Because they are gloomy holidays."

They would probably be equally impressed with Chanukah and Passover if these Jewish holidays were given public expression in the Soviet Union through mass seders or through Chanukah concerts. But they would not even consider these holidays as being religious; they would consider them as commemorating events of Jewish history which led to Jewish freedom. This is how they understand Jewishness. In their view, mixed marriages do not minimize such Jewishness.

♦ ♦ ♦ 16

Moscow and Israel

Israel IS A DIRTY WORD in the Soviet Union. One can feel that the moment one sets foot on Soviet soil. Pick up a Soviet publication—any Soviet publication in any language —and you inevitably find it contains a vitriolic article against Israel. The Soviet press, beginning with *Pravda* and *Izvestia* in Moscow, to the smallest provincial newspaper, does not tire of its anti-Israel propaganda campaign. Nor does the Soviet radio. Most emphatically, Israel is presented as "the enemy."

It is, therefore, no wonder that many Jews in the Soviet Union fear to mention the word "Israel" even when talking among themselves. Non-Jews avoid any discussion on the subject of Israel. However, a high Soviet official with whom I talked over various matters affecting Jewish life in the Soviet Union unexpectedly found himself involved in a discussion with me on the Soviet stand against Israel.

It all started when the official began to criticize American Jewry. He received me as an American journalist and displayed particular interest as to what I intended to write about my visit to the Soviet Union.

"You American Jews," he said, "are terribly anti-Soviet. You conduct a bitter campaign against us!"

This opened the door for me to raise the sensitive subject of Soviet treatment of Israel.

"American Jews," I retorted, "have good reason to be anti-Soviet. They lost six million people in Europe under the Nazi regime and they do not want to lose three million more Jews in Israel. The Arabs are at war with Israel and your government is helping them. The Arabs threaten to annihilate Israel and you send them modern weapons. You also send them instructors to train them to do the job. Your newspapers are full of venom against Israel and your radio does not miss the slightest opportunity to poison the minds of the Soviet people against Israel. Your diplomats at the United Nations deliver aggressive speeches against Israel. Do you seriously expect the Jews in the United States to like you for all this?"

The official was taken aback by the tone in which I spoke. It was obvious that he realized he had made a tactical mistake by criticizing American Jewry and thereby giving me the opportunity to start a discussion on Israel, in defense of the anti-Soviet feelings among the Jews in the United States. He knew that I would write about our conversation, and I knew that he would report it to high Soviet quarters.

"It is not true that we want to help the Arabs annihilate Israel," he asserted. "In fact, I can let you know right here that we are preparing plans to secure the existence of Israel. We now have a plan to guarantee Israel's borders."

"I know about this plan!" was my reply. "I heard about it prior to my departure for the Soviet Union. This is not a plan that Israel—or even the United States—can accept. You suggest the protection of Israel's borders. However, the question is: What borders? Do you have in mind borders that will provide security for Israel or borders which will reduce Israel and put her in permanent danger?"

The high Soviet official was astonished.

"Whatever our plan is," he argued, "doesn't it show that we don't want to annihilate Israel? Doesn't it show that we want Israel to exist?"

I admitted that there was a certain amount of logic in his argument, but went on to say that the point which he advanced did not concur with the anti-Israel propaganda in the Soviet press and with the anti-Israel orations of Soviet delegates at United Nations meetings.

"The fact is," I pointed out, "your government broke off diplomatic relations with Israel, declaring it an 'enemy country.' The fact is also that your government has stimulated other Communist governments to do the same, inspiring the Polish authorities to release a flood of vile propaganda against all the Jews of Poland."

The Soviet official became somewhat relaxed.

"You can rest assured," he said to me in a meaningful tone, "that our diplomatic relations with Israel may be resumed sooner than you think."

I did not believe him and I continued my offensive.

"In the meantime," I said, "you don't permit the emigration of Jews from the Soviet Union to Israel for reunification with their families there, in spite of the promise by your Premier Kosygin."

"This, too, may be changed very soon," he replied carefully. There was a tone of mystery in his reply.

When I left this official, I had the feeling that the Soviet Government was quite sensitive to Jewish criticism abroad.

Later I was in a position to check—under free circumstances—important facts which that Soviet official had revealed to me. I found some of them questionable, but others were correct.

In concluding my conversation with the official I pointed out to him that as long as the anti-Israel propaganda did not cease in the Soviet newspapers he should not expect any change in the anti-Soviet attitude of American Jewry, which, I stressed, is also deeply interested in securing equal rights for Jews in the Soviet Union in the areas of religion, Jewish culture, advanced general education, and the promotion of Jews to the higher governmental positions to which they are properly entitled.

Unlike in Poland, where the anti-Israel propaganda has assumed a generally anti-Jewish character of the worst kind, resulting in a panic among all elements of Jews in the country

—even among Communists who are Jews—in the Soviet Union the anti-Israel propaganda has had no such effect. The incitement against Israel in the Soviet press is vicious, but the non-Jewish population seems indifferent to it, and the authorities are apparently careful to avoid linking Soviet Jewry to the Arab-Israeli issue. This does not, however, minimize the fact that the Jews in the Soviet Union are frightened.

In 1947—a year before the establishment of the State of Israel—the Soviet Government strongly supported efforts at the United Nations to have Palestine partitioned into two separate states: one Jewish, the other Arab. When Israel was, in May 1948, proclaimed an independent state within the partitioned Palestine, the Soviet Union lost no time and was the first country to extend full diplomatic *de jure* recognition to the State of Israel.

It was no small surprise to me when Semyon Tzarapkin, the "number-two" man in the Soviet delegation to the United Nations, indicated in the course of a conversation with me in the U.N. delegates lounge that he would not be averse to meeting Dr. Emanuel Neumann, then the president of the Zionist Organization of America. Dr. Neumann was a member of the Jewish Agency delegation which represented the world Zionist movement at the United Nations Assembly. In an address before a session of the Assembly he had advocated the idea of establishing a Jewish state in Palestine.

Many in the U.N. diplomatic lobby raised their eyebrows when they afterward saw Tzarapkin shaking hands with Dr. Neumann and publicly engaging in a friendly conversation with him despite the fact that the Zionist movement has been outlawed in the Soviet Union since the early years of the Lenin Revolution. Tzarapkin played a leading role in the Soviet delegation at the United Nations. Today he still plays a very important role in the Soviet foreign diplomatic corps.

He noticed that his conversation with Dr. Neumann was provoking attention, but he did not seem to mind it. He even agreed to pose for a photograph with Dr. Neumann and with me as a neutral person who had brought them together. The photograph later appeared in the press and in a book, *Partners in State-Building*, written by the United Nations historian, Dr. Jacob A. Rubin, and published by the Diplomatic Press, Inc., of New York.

The Tzarapkin-Neumann handshaking meeting was taken by United Nations diplomats to mean that the mood in the Kremlin had suddenly become pro-Zionist after the many years of attacking Zionism as "a tool of British imperialism." This was the first public indication given on the premises of the United Nations of what the Soviet stand would be when the question of partitioning Palestine into a Jewish and an Arab state came up for a vote at the United Nations Assembly.

Then, on May 14, 1947, came an even greater surprise—the unexpected speech at a session of the Assembly by Andrei Gromyko, leader of the Soviet delegation to the United Nations, in which he bluntly announced that Moscow would favor the establishment of a Jewish state in a partitioned Palestine. This was a complete contradiction of the clearly and explicitly expressed anti-Zionist attitude voiced by Moscow for years at every possible opportunity. Mr. Gromyko referred to the tribulations of the Jewish people and to their right to have a land of their own. He said: "The fact that not one West European country was in a position to guarantee the elementary rights of the Jewish people explains the aspirations of Jews to create a state of their own. It would be unjust, taking into consideration the sufferings of the Jewish people during the war, to disclaim that right."

A year later, almost to the day, on May 18, 1948—four days following the proclamation of Israel as an independent state and after the regular troops from several Arab countries began their joint war against Israel—Gromyko was heard expressing Soviet solicitude for the Israelis. Two days later, Soviet delegate Vasily Tarasenko criticized Egypt and Jordan at the United Nations Security Council for having sent their troops into war against Israel. The Soviet organ, *Novoye Vremya*, did not hesitate to term the Arab war against Israel an act of aggression.

From May 1948 until the middle of 1950, when Israeli relations with Moscow visibly deteriorated, the Czechoslovak Government—with the approval of Moscow—was the major source of military supplies to Israel. In 1948 alone Czech exports to Israel had a total value of more than $16 million. Included were military airplanes, machine guns, rifles, and ammunition. Czechoslovakia also quietly trained groups of young Israeli Army officers at remote Czech military training camps where the Israelis were given intensive courses in aviation, communications, and parachuting. Mordecai Hod, Israel's present Air Force Commander, was one of the Israelis who received fighter pilot's training in Czechoslovakia.

Relations between Moscow and Israel began to cool off about six months after the establishment of the Jewish state, when Moscow realized that Israel would not help to promote Soviet interests in the Middle East. As time went on, friendly references to Israel ceased in the Soviet press. Instead, the tone in the Soviet press escalated from one of reserve to that of outright hostility. Gradually, Soviet diplomats in the Middle East began to make attempts to erase among Arabs recollections of the leading role the Soviet Union had played in the establishment of Israel.

In the middle of 1950 relations between the Soviet Government and Israel grew more and more hostile, culminating in the notorious Slansky Trial in Prague, and in the purge of high-ranking Jewish members of the Czech Communist Party. The next Czech arms agreement was negotiated with Nasser's Egypt. The Soviet line on Israel had swung to the other extreme. Early in 1953 Moscow severed diplomatic relations with Israel. The ostensible reason was that a bomb had been exploded at the Soviet Embassy in Tel Aviv. But this was regarded merely as a convenient excuse to end a diplomatic relationship which Stalin no longer wanted.

Diplomatic relations between the two countries were resumed after Stalin's death in 1953 but the Soviet attitude toward Israel remained rigidly unfriendly. It became outspokenly anti-Israel and pro-Arab following the Suez episode in 1956, when the Soviet Union obtained a foothold in the Middle East through Egyptian Premier Nasser. Today the Kremlin not only no longer maintains diplomatic relations with Israel but it is also providing billions of dollars' worth of modern military equipment along with Soviet instructors to Egypt and other Arab countries, encouraging them in the war against Israel.

Why? . . . Why did the Kremlin change its originally friendly policy toward Israel to a policy of animosity just a few months after the birth of the State of Israel which the Soviet Government had helped to bring about in the United Nations?

Twenty-five years ago, soon after the formation of the United Nations at the historic conclave in the San Francisco Opera House, I was invited by a member of the Truman Cabinet to come from New York to Washington and give him my evaluation of the San Francisco parley, which I had attended as an accredited journalist.

The Cabinet member was interested in my views on various aspects of the San Francisco gathering. During the course of our hour-long conversation he also wanted to know to what extent I was impressed with the stand enunciated at the San Francisco conference by Soviet Foreign Minister Vyacheslav Molotov on a number of problems.

Molotov delivered his speeches at the San Francisco conference in Russian, and they were translated on the spot into English. But the nuances of certain Russian words are not conveyed in full when these words are presented in the English translation. "Colonialism" is one such word. In English, "colonialism" has for years been an accepted term which implied no offense. Part and parcel of the British Government system was its Colonial Office, headed by a member of the Cabinet who carried the title of Colonial Secretary. The world press and the diplomatic world spoke of the Colonial Office and its functions in the same vein as they spoke of the British Foreign Office. Nothing reprehensible was seen in the colonial systems of Britain, France, Holland, and other countries, although these countries were criticized from time to time for certain acts in this or the other colonial territory.

In the terminology of the Soviet Union, however, the word "colonialism" carries an openly accusatory connotation. It implies the enslaving of the people by ruling over their lands. Under the Czarist system, the people of Bukhara, Tadjikstan, Uzbekistan, Turkestan, Kazakhstan, and other territories all the way from Tashkent to Mongolia and Afghanistan— where tens of millions of Moslems live—were considered a population of colonial territories. The Czarist authorities hardly permitted foreigners to visit these sections of the Russian Empire. Even Russians could not proceed beyond the city of Tashkent without a special permit. This system has been taken over by the Soviet regime. However, under the Soviet system these territories were proclaimed Soviet Republics which, at the same time, remained an integral part of the U.S.S.R. They are today nominally independent, although they are actually ruled from Moscow.

When Soviet Minister Molotov spoke at the first United Nations conclave in San Francisco, he made it a point to emphasize again and again that the Soviet Government's ambition would be—now that World War II was over—to energetically fight "colonialism." From the tone of his addresses when he spoke in Russian and kept repeating his attacks on "colonialism," it was obvious that the Soviet policy from then on would be to concentrate on breaking up the British Empire by causing trouble for Britain in her colonial territories. This was probably also understood by members of the British delegation at San Francisco when they heard Molotov's speeches in English translation. However, it went unnoticed by most of the delegates, to whom "colonialism" meant just another word in the Soviet propaganda vocabulary. Nor was proper attention paid by the Americans either, to Molotov's persistent reference to the need "of putting an end to colonialism," since the United States is not a colonial-minded country and the word "colonialism" was practically alien to the American people.

In my discussion with the member of the Truman Cabinet on the Soviet views outlined at San Francisco, I pointed out that the key to Soviet postwar policy on international affairs seemed to me to lie in the frank warning by Molotov that Moscow is bent on effectively fighting colonialism. It was obvious from the Soviet stand during the deliberations at San Francisco, I said, that Moscow considers that after the war only two big powers remained in the world against which the Soviet regime must stand on guard—the United States and Britain.

Discounting France as no longer a great power, the Kremlin seemed determined also to eliminate Britain as a power by concentrated action against "colonialism" and by stimulating "liberation" of the colonial territories, thereby undermining the entire structure of the British Empire.

I then pointed out to the United States Cabinet member that while the Kremlin could not afford to take on a fight against Britain and the United States simultaneously, the Soviet Government might be dormant for a number of years in its tactics against the United States but would definitely intensify its activities against Britain in the international field, with the strong determination to dissipate her colonial power in the Middle East, India, and other parts of the world and reduce her to a country limited to ruling over the British Isles only. When Moscow was sure that Britain was no longer one of the major powers, the Soviet Government would begin action against the United States. There would then be only two big powers in the world—the United States and the Soviet Union, I concluded. Nobody at that time visualized the possibility of Red China's also emerging as a power, and particularly as an anti-Moscow power.

The Soviet determination to bring about the decline of British "colonialism" suddenly found an open door for itself at the United Nations when the Palestine issue was raised there by Britain in 1947. British Prime Minister Ernest Bevin was firmly opposed to a United States recommendation to admit to Palestine even one hundred thousand Jewish survivors of the Nazi extermination camps. In the Mediterranean the British fleet was hunting down ships carrying Jewish refugees and turning them away from the Palestine shores. One such ship was sunk with all the people she carried. Refugees on other intercepted ships were interned by the British in camps on Cyprus. The matter attracted worldwide attention and was thrown by Britain onto the lap of the United Nations. This played very well into the hands of Moscow. Soviet leaders saw a good possibility to start forcing Britain from one of its positions in the Middle East—from Palestine. They not only startled the world by voting in favor of the establishment of a Jewish state in a Palestine to be freed from British administration, but they actually helped to provide Israel with military strength to withstand the onslaught of the neighboring Arab countries and to come out victorious in the first round of the Arab-Israeli war.

It did not take long for the British, once they lost their hold in Palestine, to also lose their years-long dominant positions in Egypt and Iraq and even to be told later by the weak British-educated Jordanian ruler, King Hussein, that British military advisers were no longer wanted in Jordan. Little by little Britain was forced to move out from the Arab countries and others in the Middle and the Far East where she had been the unchallenged power for many years. She is now about to leave the oil-rich protectorates of Kuwait and the Persian Gulf—her last places of influence in the Middle East. The Soviet ambition to see British "colonialism" erased from the Middle East has been realized. And not only from the Middle East.

It did not, however, take the Moscow leaders long to realize that while their strategy in voting for the establishment of Israel produced good tactical results in their short-term strategy by also stimulating Arab countries to oust Britain from their territories, the newly established Jewish state was more pro-American and pro-Western than pro-Soviet.

Certain that they had nothing to gain from Israel toward their long-cherished ambition to penetrate into the Middle East—and that Israel would never be a puppet of Moscow —the Kremlin switched around and became pro-Arab and, especially, pro-Egypt. In this, United States Secretary of State John Foster Dulles unwittingly played no small role. It was he who brought about the penetration of Soviet influence into the strategic Middle East to which Russia—even Czarist Russia

—had never had access. He capriciously rescinded, in 1956, the United States offer to Egypt of a loan toward the building of the Aswan Dam. Egyptian ruler Nasser replied to this move by nationalizing the Suez Canal and by turning to Moscow for the loan.

The Kremlin was only too happy to give Egypt the loan. It saw in this its first chance to obtain a foothold in the Middle East. The Soviet leaders started by sending several thousand experts to help in the building of the Aswan Dam; gradually they also moved in with military aid and with several thousand military "experts," including fliers, whom one can find in Egpyt today.

To make the situation even worse, Secretary Dulles influenced President Eisenhower to exercise the strongest pressure possible on the British, French, and Israeli governments, forcing them to withdraw the troops which they had sent jointly to the Suez Canal to recover it for the international ownership which had built this very important international waterway to link Europe with the Middle East and the Orient. The troops were already close to the Canal and on the verge of recapturing it but were forced to withdraw under strong American pressure, thus preventing the fall of Nasser and the recovery of the Suez Canal. After that, Nasser became even more pro-Soviet and opened the gates of the Middle East for Soviet troops and military ships. He also permitted Soviet battleships to anchor in Egyptian ports on the Mediterranean, giving Russia, for the first time in history, the opportunity to navigate its naval battle forces in the waters of the Mediterranean.

Today the Soviet Union is firmly positioned in the Mediterranean with dozens of modern battleships and submarines as a challenge to the United States Sixth Fleet there. The Kremlin today also practically controls the governments of Egypt, Iraq, Syria, Lybia, Sudan, and a number of other Arab countries by posing as the "defender" of these countries. It seeks to fill the vacuum which Britain left by withdrawing from the Middle East and to eventually also reach the oil-rich part of Arabia which borders on Iran, thus holding Iran "sandwiched" between Soviet territory and Soviet-controlled Arab lands. In simple words, it has not only gained important positions in the Middle East but it is also entrenching itself in these positions and is eyeing the possibility of controlling the entire Middle East in the not distant future.

Israel refused to serve Soviet interests in the Middle East. Egypt, Syria, and Iraq *are* serving the Soviet interests there. No wonder the Soviet Government is spitting fire against Israel and is sending billions of dollars' worth of modern arms to Egypt and the other Arab lands. No wonder Israel is "taboo" today in the Soviet Union. No wonder Israel is today considered by Moscow to be "the enemy."

There is also another important reason why the Kremlin turned hostile toward Israel only a short time after it strongly advocated in the United Nations the establishment of the Jewish state and provided, through Czechoslovakia, military support to the fledgling state pitted against the Arabs.

The Kremlin began to fear that the existence of Israel might evoke strong Jewish nationalist feelings among the close to three million Jews in the Soviet Union whom the Soviet Government is determined to assimilate. Stimulated by the fact that their government had openly and strongly advocated the establishment of Israel—and was the first country in the world to give it full diplomatic recognition—Jews in the Soviet Union considered it quite normal to express their elation over the fact that a Jewish state had come into existence. They saw nothing anti-Soviet in their pro-Israel expressions, since the Soviet press was at that time strongly pro-Israel.

Thousands of Jews in the Soviet Union who had relatives in Palestine and who had avoided maintaining any contact with them during all the years under the Communist regime—because of the ban on Zionism in Russia—suddenly did not hesitate to write, and even to cable, congratulations to their friends and relatives in Palestine after the Soviet press jubilantly reported the proclamation of Israel and the immediate recognition of the new state by the Kremlin. The Soviet censors, always careful about passing correspondence to Palestine, did not pose the slightest obstacle this time regarding passing the multitude of letters and cables that Jews in Russia sent to friends and family members in Israel, resuming the long-interrupted contact with them.

It did not take long to receive replies. Letters began to arrive from Israel, letters full of pride and joy and happiness. They were delivered to the addressees throughout Russia without any hindrance. They became the talk among many Jews who had never known much about Palestine or Jewish history. Soon Jews began to collect stamps from Israel, picture postcards with street scenes in Israel, and even to receive a magazine in Russian from Israel which was carefully edited not to offend the Soviet regime and merely to tell of life in the new Jewish state.

This, together with favorable reports of Soviet correspondents who flew to Israel on assignments from their newspapers and with similar reports over the Moscow radio of the developments in the new Jewish state, only encouraged Jews in the Soviet Union to be proud of Israel. Many of them were even congratulated by their non-Jewish friends in Moscow, Leningrad, and other Soviet cities on the courageous fighting which the Israelis displayed in their victories on the battlefronts over the armies from the five Arab states which surrounded them.

The climax was reached when the first Israeli Ambassador to the Soviet Union, Mrs. Golda Meir—now Israel's Prime Minister—arrived in Moscow in September 1948 to take her post there. Jews from various parts of the Soviet Union came to Moscow merely to gaze enthusiastically at the Israeli blue-white flag flying over the building of the embassy. They would walk past the building several times as if they were passing a shrine. Only in front of the Lenin Tomb on the Red Square could one see people displaying such reverence as that which was displayed by Jews who came to see the building assigned by the Soviet authorities to the Israeli Embassy. They looked with admiration at the signs in Hebrew and in Russian at the entrance to the embassy and at the national Jewish flag waving there.

Then came Mrs. Golda Meir's first visit to the Moscow Choral Synagogue, to attend Rosh Hashonah services. Here the feelings of Soviet Jews for Israel broke into an unprecedented open-air demonstration. Approximately forty thousand Moscow Jews appeared outside the synagogue building to hail Mrs. Meir. The synagogue usually takes in about two thousand persons. The huge crowds overflowed the adjoining streets and a sea of people engulfed Mrs. Meir when she arrived at the synagogue with members of the embassy staff. The crowds were not afraid to show their elation. There were among them many thousands of young people and Red Army officers and soldiers in uniform.

This was the first spontaneous non-Soviet open-air demonstration ever to take place in the Soviet capital. The Soviet authorities were taken aback. They had not anticipated any such demonstration and no police arrangements had been made. However, the demonstration was orderly, since by no means intended against the government, but was merely as an expression of love for Israel and its first ambassador.

Soon after this, however, few dared to raise their heads when the Israelis came to synagogue services. The tone in the Kremlin had changed not only with regard to Israel but also with regard to Soviet Jewry. Stalin, who had by that time already openly displayed anti-Jewish feelings, had obviously taken notice of the affinity which thousands of Jews displayed in Moscow toward the Israeli Ambassador. From his point of view these Jews had displayed abnormal interest in Israel. Having come to the conclusion that Israel would not become pro-Soviet and considering Israel now as being pro-American —which was worse to the Kremlin at that time than being pro-British—Stalin also became suspicious of Soviet Jewry. To him, contact of Soviet Jews with Israel was a sign of "cosmopolitanism," which he regarded as bordering on treason.

Suddenly the Soviet press began a campaign against "cosmopolitanism," which was unmistakenly taken by many to be a campaign against Jews. The first to come out with an article warning Jews against "cosmopolitanism" was Ilya Ehrenburg, the Soviet Jewish writer who never failed to sense Stalin's sentiments. In his article published in *Pravda* on September 21, 1948, Ehrenburg blasted Zionism and warned Soviet Jews against misunderstanding the recognition of Israel by the Soviet Government. This was considered a signal for Jews in Russia to cease contact with Israel and to stay away from the Israeli diplomats in the Soviet Union. After this article appeared not a soul ventured to approach the Israelis even at the Moscow Yiddish Theater where they had been enthusiastically surrounded during intermissions since the first week of the opening of the Israeli Embassy in Moscow.

Soviet hostility against Israel had started. The honeymoon period was over. It had lasted for about four months after the proclaiming of the State of Israel on May 14, 1948. Diplomatic relations continued to be maintained with Israel by Moscow, but they were cool until they were broken off, the first time in 1953 and later—for the second time—after the Arab-Israeli Six Day War in June 1967. By that time the Soviet Government stood fully on the side of the Arabs, supplying them with hundreds of tanks, planes, and other modern military equipment. From June 1967 on, the Soviet propaganda machine has been working overtime against Israel on all fronts—in the press, on the radio, in special pamphlets, and at all the sessions of the United Nations.

The high Soviet official with whom I discussed in Moscow the present animosity of the Soviet Government toward Israel indicated that "serious consideration" is now being given in the Kremlin to certain aspects of the Arab-Israeli problem. He did not go into any details. From the continued vitriolic anti-Israeli propaganda in the Soviet press it is obvious that the Kremlin "consideration" goes only in one direction— to bring Israel to a point of submission to peace on Soviet terms.

The Soviet Government is going through the motions of having the Big Four—the United States, the Soviet Union, Britain, and France—jointly impose conditions on Israel in order to reach Arab-Israeli understanding. But studying the Soviet moves on the spot in Moscow, one must come to the conclusion that the Kremlin has in fact no intention of accepting the views of the United States, or of the government of any country, with regard to Israel except its own. No matter what proposals the United States—or Britain and France—may submit on the Arab-Israeli conflict, the Soviet Government will not accept them unless they fit the Soviet pattern for the Middle East.

The Soviet pattern for the Middle East—as I could sense in talks in Moscow—is not to annihilate Israel. The existence of Israel is too important to the Kremlin if it is to maintain its control over the Arab rulers. What the Kremlin wants is to have an Israel submissive to Moscow's demands.

The Kremlin anticipates the fall of the present regime in Jordan and growing internal trouble in Lebanon. These are the only two Arab countries neighboring Israel which are not under Soviet influence, although they are at war with Israel. With a certain degree of patience, and through subversive manipulations, Moscow hopes that the march of events will also bring these two countries closer to the Soviet Government. In Jordan, King Hussein is in constant danger of losing his throne. In Lebanon, the population is split on political matters.

Should this happen, Israel would be surrounded not merely by Arab countries but by pro-Soviet Arab countries. It will be then that Moscow will intensify its efforts to achieve the kind of peace that will not be effected by any of the Big Powers but by Moscow alone. The Kremlin will simply tell Israel that the Soviet Union is the only power in a position to influence the Arabs to conclude peace with Israel. However, it will emphasize that if Israel wishes to survive she must submit to Moscow's conditions. What these conditions will be is the Kremlin's big secret today. This is probably what the high Soviet official meant when he told me that "serious consideration" is now going on in the Kremlin with regard to Israel.

It stands to reason that the Israeli Government will not permit Moscow to blackmail her. But in order to stand firm Israel must get proper aid from the United States. Today Israel is justifiably called "the bastion of world democracy" in the Middle East. It is surrounded by hostile Arab countries on land, but its shores remain open and its sky lanes are free for contact with the world. It is in the interests of the United

States—to the Sixth Fleet in the Mediterranean as well as to United States oil interests in the Middle East—that Israel's resistance vis-à-vis Soviet intentions be strengthened. It is also in the interests of the United States to realize that while Moscow goes through the motions of discussing the Middle East situation with the United States, England, and France, it has its own plans up its sleeve. Not only Israel must be on the alert concerning these plans, but also the United States, if Washington does not want to be outmaneuvered by Moscow.

... 17

With Arab Students in Moscow: Trained for What?

THE RESTAURANT IN THE Metropole Hotel in Moscow functions primarily for foreigners. At the tables there you can find American tourists, foreign diplomats, uniformed fliers of incoming airplanes from foreign countries, nationals from many lands.

You can also find young Arabs there.

I sit at a table all by myself, giving my order to the waiter in Russian. A young man who has just come in looks around for a seat and approaches my table. In the Soviet Union—as in a number of East and West European countries—a stranger may join you at your table if seats there are free. The young man obviously has noted that I am the only guest at a table for four and has decided to join me. He overheard me speaking to the waiter in Russian, so he in turn addressed me in Russian: "May I sit at your table?"

The young man had a pleasant appearance and was neatly dressed. His Russian had a slight foreign accent but sounded very elegant. I tell him that he is welcome, but I warn him that I am a foreigner, in case he is a Soviet citizen and prefers not to sit with a foreigner.

"I am a foreigner myself," he smiled, and took his seat. He started studying the menu—which is printed in both Russian and English—and when the waiter came he placed his order in Russian. He waited until the waiter had left our table and then turned to me in perfect English: "Shall we make conversation in Russian or in English? I assume that you are an American, and I overheard you addressing the waiter in Russian. I speak both languages fluently, and I judge that you probably speak more than these two languages. However, I am certain that my mother tongue is alien to you."

"And what is your mother tongue?"

"My native language," he replied in Russian, "is Arabic."

He looked to me about twenty-five years of age. I could see that he was eager to talk. He volunteered the information that he had been living in the Soviet Union for more than a year and was one of a group selected in his country to study in Moscow. He and the entire group were to be fully maintained by Soviet funds until they graduated and returned to their land, he said.

"Do you mean to say that within only one year you learned to speak Russian so fluently?" I expressed my surprise. "The Russian language is not easy to learn, yet I detect in your use of it a very profound knowledge of grammar. You also have some fine literary expressions. All this in one year?"

The young Arab seemed to be delighted by my compliment.

"This," he said, "is due to the fact that the first year of our study is devoted primarily to the acquisition of an excellent knowledge of the Russian language. After we have mastered the language, we embark on studying other subjects."

"What kind of subjects?" I was curious, having in mind advanced sciences.

"The subjects we study after we learn to speak Russian are top secret," he said in a lowered tone. "All I can tell you is that they deal with military knowledge. After four or five years of study we return to our native lands well qualified to assume important military positions."

He then dropped the subject. I was glad he did. I was not interested in the details of his training. It is well known that the Soviet Government trains Arabs in Moscow for propaganda purposes and for military activities in their countries. As if reading my thoughts, my table acquaintance switched to a theme on which Arab propagandists like to talk to foreigners.

"You read Russian," he said to me, "so you undoubtedly know from the Moscow press how strongly our Arab youth desire to liberate Palestine from the Jews. I fervently hope that we will achieve our aim. The Soviet Government is helping us very much in our ambition. This is the chief reason I and my comrades are in the Soviet Union now."

He knew that I was a foreigner. But I did not tell him that I was a Jew. I realized that he was only beginning his talk on the subject of Israel, which I did not feel like discussing with him. So I diverted the conversation diplomatically to a different and neutral subject. I asked him whether he knew Russian literature as well as he knew the language.

He was proud that I asked him this question. It gave him the opportunity to show off how much at home he was with the Russian classics as well as with the modern Soviet writers.

"I have read all the works of Leo Tolstoy, Maxim Gorky, Feodor Dostoevsky, and have studied the works of the modern great writers—Mikhail Sholokhov, Alexander Fadyeev, and others. I know the poetry of Pushkin and Lermontov and I enjoy it no less than the modern poets Yevtushenko and Voznesensky," he said proudly.

This gave me the opportunity to continue our conversation on literary rather than on political subjects. The waiter brought our food, and our conversation was interrupted, to my great satisfaction. I started to eat.

I was willing to indulge in eating rather than in conversation, but not so my young Arab. He wanted to know what city I lived in, and when I told him that I live in New York, he was curious to know how it was that one who lives in the United States knows Russian literature—the old and the new—as well as I do.

I explained to him that almost all American universities offer courses in Russian literature. I added that I am a Russian-born who came to the United States at an early age and that I am still interested in literary developments in Russia. He then wanted to know whether I was a member of the literary profession.

"I am a journalist," I informed him. "At one time I was stationed in Moscow as an American correspondent. I have also been stationed in other countries."

He suddenly became excited.

"Then you have really mastered quite a number of languages!" he said in a tone of youthful envy.

I told him that I know about ten languages, some of them better, some not so perfectly, and that with the knowledge of these languages I cannot get lost in any country of the world. He was looking up to me in a kind of admiration which soon, however, disappeared, his face becoming very serious:

"Don't you think it would have been better for our world if all the people spoke one universal language?" he asked gloomily.

I agreed with him, but pointed out that this would never happen as long as each nation had its own culture and endeavored to develop it through its own language.

"Incidentally," I added, "there are universal languages which cultural people throughout the world use in their daily life."

"You mean Esperanto?" he asked.

"No," I answered, "I mean the language of music, the language of chemistry, the language of physics. The entire musical world, in all the countries of the world, reads and uses the same musical notes as the only musical alphabet and the only language of music for all interested in music. And the same is true with scientists all over the world. The languages of chemistry and physics are for them the same in all countries."

I could see that my young acquaintance was impressed. It was obvious that I had implanted a new thought in his mind.

"You are quite right," he said to me after a minute of reflection. "It never occurred to me before to think in these terms about music and science."

We continued our conversation at the table long after the dinner was over. We spoke on many subjects, none political.

The young Arab became so attached to me that he wanted to order drinks so that our occupying the table should be justified in the eyes of the management of the restaurant. However, I told him that time did not permit my spending the entire evening in the restaurant, and he understood.

"Then may I look for another opportunity to join you here?" he asked. "Perhaps for dinner tomorrow? I learned so much from you tonight in such a short time!"

He sounded genuinely grateful.

"If it is no imposition," he continued, "I would like to invite you to our dormitory to meet the other students from my country. They will all be eager to listen to you after I report to them about our conversation here tonight."

Without waiting for my answer he took a piece of paper from a notebook in his pocket and jotted down the address of the dormitory. He also jotted down his name—a real Arabic name. I looked at the address and noted that it was the location of a military installation. I was surprised that he had extended the invitation to this place to me and that he had written down the address in his own handwriting, giving all the details without knowing who I was.

It was not my intention to visit military installations in the Soviet Union. The young Arab had obviously been swept away by some new thoughts that had impressed him in our conversation, but he had no right to reveal to me, a foreigner, the location of the place where he and others like him were being trained. As for my part, I had no desire even to be suspected of seeking information on the training of Arabs in the Soviet Union.

I politely declined his invitation by explaining to him that I would remain in Moscow only for three more days and that my timetable for those days did not permit me to visit him and meet his colleagues, since the dormitory—as could be seen from the address—is located in a remote part of Moscow.

"If that is the case, then at least permit me to bring some of my friends to the restaurant here tomorrow evening to meet you," he begged. "You don't have to have dinner with us if your time is limited, but we could order a drink as we sit together at one table exchanging questions and answers for an hour or so. My friends, I am sure, will learn very much from you in one hour, as I did tonight during our talk."

The next evening, shortly before theater time, I walked into the restaurant and noticed a group of six young Arabs sitting at a table, my young acquaintance among them. He rose from the table to greet me and to escort me to the seat which had been reserved for me among his friends.

They were all youths of student age and each of them spoke fluent Russian. From time to time they exchanged remarks in Arabic, but this was more a matter of habit than of trying to talk on matters they did not want me to understand. A large bottle of French cognac was on the table, signifying to the holiday spirit of the meeting. French cognac is a very expensive drink in the Soviet Union and is served only on special occasions.

"And I thought that the Moslem religion forbids the drinking of liquor," I remarked jokingly when we took the first drink, toasting to "peace in this world."

"Who told you we were religious?" the young Arab of the night before, who acted as spokesman for the group, asked sarcastically. "In Moscow do as the Russians do. Drink wine, drink vodka, drink cognac. The drinking of cognac is to us an expression of friendship."

I spent with the group the promised hour prior to my leaving for the Bolshoi Theater to see an excellent performance there of Mozart's *The Marriage of Figaro.* It was directed by the Jewish conductor Boris Chaikin, who was enthusiastically applauded by the audience at the end of each act.

The group, it turned out, did not impress me as being as intelligent as their spokesman of the previous evening. It is one thing to find yourself in the company of one Arab in Moscow and it is quite a different thing to conduct a conversation with a group of Arabs who you know are being trained there for certain purposes. Meeting with the group in so public a place as a restaurant also had much to do with the fact that there was really no inspiring exchange of views between them and me.

When I took leave of the group, their spokesman escorted me from the restaurant to the exit. I said to him half-seriously, half-jokingly: "Where do poor Arab students in Moscow get the money to patronize such an expensive restaurant as the one in Hotel Metropole?"

The answer was very instructive.

"We don't have the money to come here every evening," he said. "However, it is very monotonous to carry an intensive study load and to spend the rest of the time in the gray atmosphere of our dormitory. So, what happens? We save up our money in order to indulge from time to time in eating in a good restaurant, in a pleasant atmosphere, among well-dressed people, enjoying good food, good entertainers, and the lively music of a good orchestra.

"This," he continued, "helps our morale. Our Soviet instructors understand this and occasionally permit us to have a free evening and a good time outside the dormitory. This is not only good for our morale, but it also is helpful to the purposes of our studies here. Take, for instance, my meeting here with you last night. It elevated me spiritually and was quite refreshing after long hours of training during the day and long, monotonous evenings in the dormitory."

"But are you sure that you were not watched while sitting and talking to me such a long time in the restaurant?" I asked. "Are you sure that your entire group was not watched here tonight, sitting in such a public place as the restaurant and conducting a discussion with a foreigner who is an American journalist?"

"It is quite possible that you are right," was his reply. "There is an element of suspicion that we may have been watched. It is even possible that we may be reprimanded in a day or two for meeting with you. But nothing serious will happen either to me or to my comrades, since we are not going to see you again. We are here for a purpose and the Soviet authorities know that we are dedicated to our purpose.

Talks with foreigners only enhance our knowledge. And, after all, we are not Russians. We are foreigners ourselves and therefore can afford to permit ourselves certain things which Russians would hesitate to do."

I could see that he was eager to talk with me longer. But he could not stay away long from his friends and I was afraid I might be late for the opera. So we parted with a friendly handshake.

"You have my address," he said when parting, "and I am going to stay here three or four years more. So if you happen to visit Moscow again, drop me a postcard and I will come to visit you at whatever hotel you are staying. Don't worry about the consequences such a visit might have for me with the Soviet authorities. If I don't worry, you need not have any worry either."

He indicated to me that he is the son of an Arab school teacher and that the other Arab students in his group are all from educated families. They are all extremists and were therefore selected by Soviet "educators" to be brought to Moscow for training in the Soviet Union. They are only one of the groups of young men whom the Soviet Government brings to Moscow from countries in Asia and Africa to be indoctrinated with the Communist spirit, which they are to implant in their native lands upon their return home.

Strangely enough, these young Arabs are not at all popular in Moscow and are visibly avoided by Russians, including the Russian students. This is because the Russian people dislike Indians, Arabs, and Africans. Despite the military aid which the Soviet Government gives to the Arab countries in their war against Israel—and notwithstanding the strong pro-Arab and anti-Israel propaganda of the Soviet press and radio—Arabs in Moscow are looked upon by the Russians as being an inferior element.

The hostile feeling of the general population toward the Arabs emanates to a great extent from the fact that the people in the Soviet Union resent the sending by their government of billions of dollars' worth of Soviet-made products to the Arab countries.

This sentiment is so pronounced that the Soviet press has discontinued the publication of photographs showing the loading of Soviet ships and planes with cargo destined for Arab lands. Instead of evoking pride that the Soviet Union is in a position to aid friendly countries, these photos provoke indignation among the Soviet masses, who are finding it very difficult to buy shoes, clothing, certain foodstuffs, and other prime necessities. The feeling of the average Russian is that if the Kremlin were not sending such huge quantities of military and civilian materials to the Arab countries life would be much easier for the average family in the Soviet Union.

Ignored by the Russian youth and isolated in separate dormitories, the Arab and African students who are brought over from their countries to study in Moscow feel very lonely. Thus they seek distraction in the lobbies and in the restaurants of the hotels for foreigners. They seek foreign atmosphere. A visit to the Metropole Hotel is for every one of them a refreshing event, especially if he is fortunate enough to get into a conversation with an American, as was the case with the young Arab who did not disguise his enthusiasm about meeting me.

··· 18

Will the Word "Jew" Be Abolished from Jewish Identity Documents?

WILL THE SOVIET GOVERNMENT ever eliminate the word "Jew" from the identification documents of its Jewish citizens?

This question, when posed to Soviet officials, is very embarrassing to them. They know that the marking of documents with the word "Jew" makes it difficult for Jews to secure proper employment and hinders their entrance to schools of higher learning. They are aware of the fact that anyone who is identified as a Jew in his internal passport cannot get any position in the government's foreign service or in other "sensitive" state services. Even in the Communist Party higher positions are closed to anyone who is identified in his documents as a Jew, no matter how long he has been a member of the party. Soviet authorities realize that even though this may not be intended, the formal classification of Jews, not as nationals of the Soviet Republic in which they were born, but as members of a "Jewish nationality" places the Jewish population in a special category.

Lenin at one time insisted in his writings that there is no such thing as a "Jewish identity." The question as to whether Jews constitute a nationality also was openly discussed at meetings of Communist Party leaders in Moscow in the early years of the Communist Revolution. Some Communist leaders, accepting Lenin's thesis, advanced the argument that Jews in the U.S.S.R. must be considered natives of the Soviet Republics in which they were born. If they were born in Russia proper, they should be considered citizens of the Soviet Federated Russian Republic; if they were natives of the Ukraine, they should be nationals of Soviet Ukraine; if their birthplace was in Byelorussia, they should be Byelorussian nationals. Born in Lithuania, they should be Lithuanians, in Estonia, they should be Estonians, and so on.

Nowadays Soviet officials, when presented with Lenin's view and when pressed for an explanation as to why they identify the Jews not by their native Soviet territory but by their religion—in a country which combats religion—assert that Jews in the U.S.S.R. became a nationality when the government designated the remote Biro-Bidjan area in Siberia as a "Jewish Autonomous Region" intended for the settlement of Jews in a Jewish environment. But Biro-Bidjan is today hardly Jewish. Only about fifteen thousand of the three million Jews in the Soviet Union live there, and many of them are intermarried. The majority of the population of 175,000 in Biro-Bidjan is Russian and Ukrainian.

The same officials go on to explain that every citizen in the U.S.S.R. is denoted in his identity document by his nationality. If he is a Ukrainian, they point out, his document so states. If he is Armenian or Tadjik, or Lithuanian, or Latvian, his nationality is inscribed in his personal documents. Why should Jews be sensitive about their being identified as Jews in their identity papers, the officials ask.

What the officials evade answering is whether nationality is denoted by Soviet land of birth or by religion. To other nationalities the Soviet regulations apply the principle of nationality by birthplace. The Jews are the only citizens in the U.S.S.R. whose nationality is marked by their religious origin.

This despite the fact that the majority of the Jews in the Soviet Union are far from religious, especially those born since
the Communist Revolution of more than fifty years ago.

The present practice in the U.S.S.R. of indicating nationality of the Jewish population in the country by religion and
not by the name of the Soviet Republic of which they are natives very strongly resembles the practice of the Czarist regime. It was the policy of the Czarist Government to identify
residents by religion—Jews and non-Jews alike—in order
to make a distinction between Jews and non-Jews. Unlike
the non-Jews, the Jews were restricted to residence in certain areas of the country and to a quota in institutions of learning. They were barred from employment in state and
municipal institutions. Under the Czarist system, anyone
whose document indicated that he was a Jew could not serve
in the police force, or in the postal office system, or even as a
messenger in the state-owned telegraph office. Employment in
the railway system was closed to him even on the very lowest
levels—he could not even be a luggage porter at a railway
station. In the cities he could not be employed in the streetcar
system or hold a job as a municipal garbage collector. He was
taken into the armed forces for three years of active service,
but he could never be promoted, not even to the rank of sergeant.

These discriminations were abolished after the fall of the
Czarist regime, together with the practice of marking the
word "Jew" in identity documents of Jews. They were first
eliminated by the Kerensky regime, which proclaimed equal
rights for Jews. They were also declared illegal later by Lenin
when he overthrew the Kerensky Government. All anti-Jewish restrictions—residential, educational, professional—
were outlawed, including the ban on promoting Jews in the
military service to officer rank. In fact, it was Leon Trotsky, a
Jew, who organized the Red Army.

The policy of marking Jewish identity documents with the
word "Jew" was revived in the 1930's when Stalin reintro-
duced a rigorous internal passport system. It paved the way for
the later elimination of Jews from the Soviet foreign service,

from leading posts in government institutions and from higher positions in the Communist Party. It culminated in the closing down in 1948 of all Jewish cultural institutions and, later, in the mass arrests and "liquidation" of hundreds of Jewish intellectuals, among them the most renowned writers and actors. Many of them, including prominent members of the Communist Party, were sent to slave labor camps in Siberia, where they found their death under most brutal circumstances.

Although the years of anti-Jewish terror terminated with the death of Stalin, Jews in the Soviet Union today still carry the feeling of insecurity and of being considered second-class citizens because of the word "Jew" in their identity documents. They feel exposed to anti-Jewish discriminations. They feel that they are still a "distrusted element." They definitely find it more and more difficult to gain admission to schools of higher learning because the nationality of each applicant is carefully checked.

In Moscow you learn that the question of whether or not to abolish the word "Jew" from the identity documents of Jewish citizens—and apply to the latter the nationality of the republic in the U.S.S.R. of which they are natives—has recently come up for discussion in the Kremlin. High Soviet leaders are far from happy over the criticism abroad that they are promoting discrimination against Jews and thereby strengthening anti-Semitic sentiments in the country. They are beginning to feel that the system of marking the documents of Jewish citizens with the word "Jew" is creating a "Jewish problem" in the country—something which Lenin would not have tolerated.

In Moscow you also discover that when the Soviet authorities permit a "trusted" Jew to go abroad for a brief visit, or when a Jew is included in a Soviet cultural mission sent abroad, the word "Jew" is eliminated from his travel documents. In his travel passport his nationality is entered as being that of the U.S.S.R. There is no reference whatsoever to his Jewish identity. He is under instructions to state merely that he is of Soviet nationality when filling out questionnaires for immigration authorities abroad upon entering a foreign country. The same instructions also hold for him when registering in a hotel abroad. The Soviet authorities are eager to prevent people abroad from seeing that the word "Jew" appears on documents of Jewish citizens. This in itself indicates that they have a guilty feeling about marking the identity documents of Jews within the country with the word "Jew."

Why, then, do they not give up the designation "Jew" in such documents?

The answer can easily be found in a statement made by Khrushchev in 1956, when as head of the Soviet Government he received a French delegation. Replying to a question about why Jews are no longer to be found in high positions in the Soviet system, Khrushchev said: "In the early years of the Revolution there were many Jews in high positions in the government and in the party. They were better educated and, perhaps, even more revolutionary than the average Russian. With the march of time, however, we educated plenty of non-Jews so they would be capable of holding responsible positions in Soviet life. The indigenous populations would resent it strongly if Jews were to hold high positions now. This is easy to understand. There would be, for instance, great jealousy and animosity in the Ukraine if a Jew were appointed to an important post and surrounded himself with other Jews in his office."

Not only was Khrushchev, during his years of ruling, anxious to follow Stalin's policy of eliminating Jews from major positions in the Soviet Union, but he also advised other governments to do likewise. During a visit which he made to Poland in 1956 he told the leaders of the government there publicly that "there are too many Abramovitches" in high posts in Communist Poland. When he was criticized later in the Western world for his anti-Jewish outbursts, he denied that he was an anti-Semite and said that his daughter was married to a Jew—something which has never been made public in the Soviet Union.

The present Kosygin-Brezhnev Government, although realizing that it has a "Jewish problem" on its hands because of discriminating against Jews, does not, so far, deviate from Stalin's and Khrushchev's policy with regard to the Jews. When I worked in Moscow as an American correspondent in the late 1920's a good many of the high officials in the Commissariat on Foreign Affairs were Jews. The censors who watched over the cables sent by foreign correspondents were all Jews; they knew English, French, German, Italian, and other languages used by the correspondents in their dispatches to their newspapers. Many of the responsible officials of the Vneshtorg—the Soviet trading corporation doing business with the foreign countries—were Jews; they were experts in international commerce and mastered foreign languages. The heads of various departments in the State Bank were Jews; they were men with financial training.

Most of these Jews were Communists and were completely assimilated. Though mastering various languages, they could not speak or read the Jewish languages. They were not interested in anything Jewish. In fact, they looked down on those Jewish Communists who were active in developing Jewish cultural life, in those years an activity very much encouraged by the Soviet Government, which in later years suppressed it.

Today Communist Jews could not hold the kinds of positions their predecessors held. Whether they care about anything Jewish or not, their identity documents stamp them as being Jews. And this is the key to what Khrushchev meant when he explained to the French delegation the Soviet stand on Jews during the past quarter of a century. The old generation of Jewish Communists who held high posts in the state and in the party perished in the political purges which Stalin conducted or were simply removed from the positions held. They were replaced by non-Jews, no matter if the latter did not possess the requisite knowledge.

The present Kosygin-Brezhnev Government knows that the removal of Jews from positions they held, and their nonadmission to new posts for which they are qualified, is taken abroad as a sign of anti-Jewish bias, which today finds its expression in many areas of Soviet life. However, they vehemently deny the existence of such bias. They refer to the fact that the Soviet Constitution guarantees equal rights to all Soviet citizens. That their denials clash with the actual facts is obvious to any student of Soviet affairs. Khrushchev, with his peasant mentality, was courageous enough to admit this.

Contrary to the Kremlin's policy during the first years of the Soviet Revolution of encouraging Jewish cultural and national feelings among the Jewish population, the policy today is directed toward a program of forced assimilation of the Jews by suppressing Jewish cultural activities, refusing to reopen the many Jewish schools that existed in the years prior to Stalin's anti-Jewish course, opposing the reestablishment of the Jewish state theaters which were liquidated during the last years of the Stalin regime, and not even permitting the publication of a textbook of Jewish history in the Russian language.

But while eager to see the Jews assimilated, the Kremlin seems—nevertheless—to be determined to keep the word "Jew" in the identity documents of its Jewish population. The leaders of the Kremlin still fear that if the word "Jew" is prematurely eliminated from the personal documents of its Jewish citizens—and their nationality based on their native Soviet Republic, as is the case with other nationalities—the younger generations of Soviet-born Jews, constituting a most intelligent element in the country, will "penetrate" the wall that has been erected to prevent Jews from occupying high state and party positions. There is today practically no difference in appearance between the younger Jews and non-Jews; and Russian—not Yiddish—is today the language which the younger generation of Jews speaks. Take the designation "Jew" off his identity documents, and it will be practically impossible to distinguish a Jew from a Russian.

Under such circumstances, what could prevent the recurrence of a greater influx of Jews into Soviet universities if the word "Jew" disappeared from their applications? What could prevent Jews from again reaching the high positions they held in government offices, in the armed forces, and in the party apparatus during the years when no discrimination was practiced against them? What would happen to Khrushchev's theory that Jews must be prevented from occupying important posts—a theory to which the present Soviet Government subscribes?

Thus the Kremlin now faces a vicious circle. On the one hand, the leaders of the Kremlin would like to see the Jews in the U.S.S.R. completely disappear by assimilation—and they believe that this could eventually be achieved, since the older element of Jewry in the Soviet Union is dying out. On the other hand, they stubbornly stick to identifying Jews in their documents with the word "Jew," in order that the number of Jewish students in the universities remain restricted and the important state and party positions remain inaccessible to them. The fact that the outside world condemns them for the anti-Jewish restrictions may not be pleasant to the Soviet rulers. It is even embarrassing to them to have to come out ever so often with denials of the existence of such restrictions. Yet the policy of keeping the Jews under disabilities is to them a basic policy from which they seemingly will not deviate for a long time to come.

Thus the word "Jew" will, in all probability, remain in the documents of Soviet Jews despite the fact that Lenin definitely opposed the idea that there is such a thing as a "Jewish nationality," and notwithstanding the criticism from abroad—even from Communists abroad.

In March 1964, shortly before he was deposed from his post as Premier of the Soviet Union, Khrushchev indicated that the internal passport in which Jews are identified as Soviet citizens of Jewish nationality might be superseded by a "labor certification document" which would not emphasize the nationality of the holder. This would have meant that the word "Evrei" (Jew) would be eliminated from the identity documents carried by Jews. Like a number of other of Khrushchev's ideas, this one is no longer mentioned by any of the Kremlin leaders. Khrushchev's successors seemed to be little interested in his views on the modification of the internal passport as they are in his professed view that the gates of the Soviet Union should be opened to anyone who wants to leave the country.

While hoping for the assimilation of the Jews in the long run but in the meantime maintaining the word "Jew" in their personal identity documents in order to prevent their reacquiring access to high state and party positions, the Soviet Government is, without even realizing it, pushing Soviet Jews into Jewish nationalism—the very thing which the Kremlin wants to see disappear.

This is especially the case with regard to the younger elements in Soviet Jewry. The Jewish youth, not being religious and being completely alienated from Jewish culture, which is suppressed by the Soviet authorities, is beginning to wonder what the word "Jew" in their documents actually signifies. As Soviet citizens, born and raised under the Communist regime, the young Jews understand the Soviet policy with regard to national minorities as being to encourage these minorities in their national cultural aspirations.

"Why, then, is Jewish culture suppressed? Why can't we learn about our own Jewish heritage? Why is there no book on Jewish history published in the Soviet Union to tell us about our past?"

The young Jewish generation in the Soviet Union is now beginning to ask these questions and is searching for the answers. The younger Soviet-born Jew is not ashamed of being marked as a Jew and does not intend to deny his Jewishness. On the contrary, he wants now to know, what is a Jew? He wants to discover his Jewish background. This is especially true with regard to the academic youth. Inquiring minds, the Jewish students are now seeking more and more to establish the meaning of Jewishness.

Some of the younger Jews, reading about Israel in the Soviet press—which carries only propaganda inciting against Israel—are seeking to learn about Jews and Jewishness from Israeli broadcasts given in the Russian language and beamed to the Soviet Union. They clandestinely tune in on the wavelength which brings news from Israel to them. They listen to the news with utmost attention. They relay the news to others. They are inspired by the fact that there is a Jewish state with a people courageous and dedicated. They know little or nothing about the way of life in Israel, but from the meager information reaching them in the broadcasts in Russian from Israel, they feel that there is a strong meaning in being a Jew, and they want to understand this meaning of which they are so completely ignorant.

In Moscow and in other Soviet cities some of them encounter American Jews who visit the Soviet Union as tourists. They learn that Jews in the United States—and in other countries—do not have the word "Jew" in their passports, that they are classified in their documents as American nationals. They learn also that in the United States Jews are not prevented from maintaining Jewish cultural and communal institutions, Jewish schools, and even Jewish universities where ancient, modern, and contemporary Jewish history is a substantial part of the curriculum. This puzzles them even more. It is hard for them to understand why Jewish history and Jewish culture are muted in their country as part of the official policy of their government.

Because the Soviet press and radio constantly feed the Soviet population with savage propaganda against Israel, and because the Jewish youngsters know how to evaluate the maliciousness of this propaganda after listening to the broadcasts in Russian from Israel, their sympathy for Israel grows parallel with their eagerness to secure more knowledge about their own Jewishness. They would like to know how to read and to speak Yiddish. Many of them would also like to study Hebrew, the language banned in the Soviet Union.

Thus the Kremlin, through its policy of suppressing Jewish culture and by marking identity documents with the designation "Jew"—as was done by the Czarist regime—is actually driving the younger generation of Jews to Jewish nationalism. In this the Kremlin is unwittingly repeating the methods used under the Czar—methods which drove the Jews in Russia to Zionism. It is a mistake to think that modern Zionism was inspired by Dr. Theodor Herzl, a prominent Austrian Jewish journalist. Modern Zionism was born in Czarist Russia long before Dr. Herzl was aware of it. It was a product of Czarist discrimination against Jews and of the pronounced anti-Semitism which made life in Czarist Russia difficult for Jews. The first organized groups of immigrants to Palestine came from no other country than Czarist Russia. Jewish nationalism was strong in Russia in the Czarist period because Jews had been eliminated from the general stream of life in that country.

The Soviet Government today, by discriminating against Jews and by singling them out in their identity documents as a special nationality—Jews are equated with Gypsies in the Soviet Encyclopedia—unconsciously follows in the Czarist path of driving into Jewish nationalism the great majority of the three million Jews in the Soviet Union, including the many who were born under the Soviet regime and know nothing of themselves as Jews.

History repeats itself in Russia today with regard to Jews. The Czarist regime also desired the assimilation of the Jews, but aimed to effect it through conversion from the Jewish religion to the Russian Orthodox religion, and failed. The Kremlin, combatting religion, hopes to assimilate the Jews through intermarriage. It permits youngsters of mixed parentage, when they reach the age of sixteen, to choose the nationality of the non-Jewish parent. But this is a long process. In the meantime Jewish consciousness is being awakened among the Jewish youth which, to all intents and purposes, is practically already assimilated but seeing the word "Jew" in its identity documents is inquisitive as to its Jewish origin. Jewish youths also become more Jewish-minded and Jewish-feeling as they begin to realize that the designation "Jew" in the Soviet identity documents actually intended to bring it about that Jews be considered second-class citizens by quietly imposing serious restrictions upon them.

• • • 19

The Outlook for Jewish Survival in the Soviet Union: Will Jews Disappear?

JEWISH LIFE IN the Soviet Union today is centered around three positions: (1) the approximately sixty synagogues throughout the country, which reflect Jewish religious existence; (2) the Yiddish monthly magazine, *Sovietish Heimland*, which represents the only expression of Jewish culture since the mass liquidation by Stalin of all Jewish cultural institutions; and (3) the Jewish youth, which knows nothing about Jewishness but is nevertheless developing a strong Jewish consciousness.

All three positions are important to Jewish survival in the U.S.S.R. However, the most important factor upon which the future of Jewish life in the Soviet Union will stand or fall is the Jewish youth. Without a youth which feels Jewish, there will be no Jewish continuity. Soviet Jewry could then—with very few exceptions—become a matter of the past in about twenty-five years. It could disappear through intermarriage and assimilation, as the Kremlin would like to see it do.

There can be no question about the need to secure equal

treatment in Russia for the Jewish religion, which is deprived of many of the privileges the Soviet Government accords to all other religions. But one must look realistically at the fact that the future of Soviet Jewry does not rest on the aged Jews who cling to the synagogue. These Jews should be given every possibility to live their lives in full accordance with their religious traditions, which are part and parcel of their existence. However, it is highly questionable that these traditions are the foundation upon which Jewish life can be built for the future. The great majority of Soviet Jewry is not religious and is not inclined to become religious.

The same thing can be said for *Sovietish Heimland*. This publication constitutes a Jewish cultural position, although it is a Communist publication, directed by a Communist editor. Its contents are—as is everything published in the Soviet Union—Communist-oriented. However, it is helping to develop new cadres of Yiddish writers to replace those brutally slain under the Stalin regime and it carries literary material of general Jewish cultural value.

But *Sovietish Heimland* is far from enough to serve as a forum for the several hundred thousands of Jews in the Soviet Union who still read Yiddish and are rooted in Jewish culture. It does not reflect the sentiments of those in the U.S.S.R. who would like to see Jewish culture restored to its full rights in the country. Although it reaches a limited number of Jews, primarily those in the territories acquired by the Soviet Union after the war where Yiddish is still spoken—the Baltic countries, Bukovina, Galicia, Carpatho-Russia—it does not reach the Jewish youth, because the Soviet-born youth cannot read Yiddish.

On the other hand, there is no doubt—as I mentioned in the previous chapter—that there is a large segment among the Soviet-born Jewish youth that is beginning to become aware of its Jewish identity and is strongly inclined to maintain this identity. These young people have no Jewish background, but are eager to acquire it. They are like grown-up orphans who know nothing about their parents and who are extremely anxious to discover any trace that may lead them to finding out who their parents were and what happened to them.

It is upon this segment that Jewish survival in the Soviet Union mainly depends.

The question thus arises: What should be done for the Soviet-born Jewish generation which is Jewish in its identity and in spirit but has no access whatsoever to any Jewish knowledge? How can Jewish content be provided to the majority of Soviet Jewry which is not interested in religion and cannot read or speak Yiddish?

The answer to this question is, I believe, in the establishment in Moscow of a Jewish weekly publication *in the Russian language*. All other national minorities in the Soviet Union have their national publications. Certainly the Jews, since they are designated by the Soviet Government as a nationality, have a justified claim to such a publication for their three million brethren, about 80 percent of whom can read no language but Russian.

A Jewish periodical in the Russian language would contribute not a little to strengthening of Jewish feelings among hundreds of thousands of Soviet Jews, young and middle-aged. The mere fact that such a publication appeared regularly every week would of itself fortify the Jewish identity sentiments among many Jews throughout the country.

I do not deceive myself by thinking that such a publication would not be Communist-directed. Everything that is printed in Russia is Communist-oriented. Just as the editor of any existing publication in the Soviet Union is a trusted member of the Communist Party, so also will be the editor of any publication in Russian intended for Jewish readers.

Nevertheless, I am certain that such a Jewish organ would also carry some material on Jewish subjects and items reflecting Jewish life, even though they would be Communist-tainted. Such a publication could become a medium to be found in countless Jewish homes in all parts of the U.S.S.R. It would not be the ideal Jewish publication from the point of view of Jews in the free world, but it would serve the purpose of fostering Jewish affinity.

A Jewish magazine in the Russian language was permitted in Moscow under the Soviet regime in the 1920's, during the period of the mass colonization of Russian Jews on land in the Crimea and in the Ukraine. In addition to having many thousands of subscribers, it was sold on newsstands in Moscow and in other cities. The *Tribuna*—that was the name of the publication—was published by the OZET, a Soviet-Jewish organization engaged in furthering settlement of declassed Jews on the land. It carried news and photos reflecting Soviet-Jewish life; its material was not restricted solely to reports on Jewish colonization; it also fought anti-Semitism and reported selected developments in Jewish life abroad. Its editor was S. Diamantstein, a top Jewish Communist leader who was close to Lenin and Stalin. He was later liquidated by Stalin. The last issue of the *Tribuna* appeared in 1933. Since then no other Russian language magazine for Jews has appeared.

There are Jews in the Soviet Union today who still remember the role played in Jewish life under the Czar by two Jewish weeklies in the Russian language. Both were published in St. Petersburg—now Leningrad—but their impact was strong upon thousands and thousands of Jews in Moscow, Odessa, Kiev, and other cities where the Jews spoke mainly Russian.

Just as today, in Czarist times many Jewish students were assimilated and could not read Yiddish. The same held for many of the top Jewish leaders in the Czarist capital and in Moscow. Vladimir Jabotinsky, for instance, was one of the young Zionist leaders who at that time could not yet read Yiddish.

To reach those Jews who could not read Yiddish, and especially the student generation, the non-Zionist leaders started to publish in St. Petersburg a weekly Russian-language magazine, *Voskhod*. It was one of the best Jewish publications in any language and became popular with thousands and thousands of Jewish families all over Russia. Impressed by the success of *Voskhod*, Zionist leaders in St. Petersburg also started publication of a weekly in the Russian language. This was the Zionist weekly, *Rassviet*, which, similarly, soon found its way into many Jewish homes all over the country. Both publications played an important role in strengthening Jewish identity among "Russified" Jews.

American Jewish leaders interested in the fate of Soviet Jewry may not know this chapter of Jewish history in Russia, when Jewish cultural needs were met in the Russian language. They should, however, take a leaf from the books of pre-Communist Jewish history in Russia, as well as from the Communist period when the *Tribuna* appeared in Moscow for Jewish readers. They can, of course, insist, as they do, on full restoration of Yiddish culture, but should also bear in mind the argument of the Soviet Government that the majority of the Jews in the U.S.S.R. do not understand Yiddish and cannot read Yiddish. This argument can only fortify the demand that the Jews in the U.S.S.R., as a nationality, should have their national cultural interests served also in Russian.

Only through a Russian-Jewish organ can the Jewish youth in the Soviet Union be reached. The key to Jewish continuity lies, therefore, very much in the establishment of a Jewish publication in the Russian language.

Another great need of the Jews in the Soviet Union if they are to survive as Jews is the publication of a Jewish history textbook in the Russian language. No such book has ever appeared in the Soviet Union. At the same time, the publication of histories of all other nationalities in the U.S.S.R. is encouraged by the Soviet authorities. Inasmuch as history is the "memory" of a nation, the three million Jews in the Soviet Union stand to become "a people without a memory" although they have a rich cultural and spiritual history several thousands of years old.

Even during the early years of the Soviet Revolution, when Yiddish cultural institutions were financed by the government and when hundreds of state-maintained Yiddish schools functioned in various parts of the country—even then Jewish history, like the Hebrew language, was banned. The very concept of "Jewish history" was taboo. Children in the Jewish schools were taught the general history of the "class struggle," in which there were sections dealing with accounts of Jewish workers fighting their "exploiters," Jewish and non-Jewish.

Thus a Jewish generation grew up in the Soviet Union without having the slightest knowledge of the Jewish past, whether of biblical times or of the later periods. Today one finds in the Soviet Union Jews of the age of fifty who are totally ignorant of anything that took place in Jewish history. They include some who may still speak and read Yiddish, which they were taught in the hundreds of Yiddish schools which existed in the early years of the Soviet regime. Also completely untutored in Jewish history is, of course, the body of Jewish student youth which has grown up during the years since the liquidation by the Soviet authorities of all Jewish cultural institutions.

There are books of Jewish history in some of the major Soviet libraries which are closed to the public. These volumes are available to scholars only and by special permit. They are "forbidden literature." The younger Jews in the Soviet Union do not even know of their existence, and even if they did they would have no access to them.

The young Jews in the Soviet Union are completely ignorant not only of their ancient history but also of the Jewish history of the Middle Ages—even of the Spanish Inquisition—as well as of contemporary Jewish history. They even know nothing about the history of the Jews in their own country, except for the general fact that Jews were oppressed under the Czarist regime. They certainly do not know that Boghdan Khmelnitsky, the great hero for whom a street right near the Moscow synagogue is named, has gone into Jewish history as one of the worst slaughterers of Jews in the Ukraine. His pogroms on Jews were fierce and barbaric.

In hiding Jewish history from Soviet Jewry, the Kremlin is seeking to confuse the Jewish youth in the Soviet Union even with regard to current Jewish historical developments. Not only is the Soviet Government giving a completely false picture about the State of Israel; it has made it its policy to present the Nazi annihilation of millions of Jews in Soviet territory during the German occupation as an event directed against "Soviet citizens," carefully omitting to mention that there were huge numbers of Jews among those citizens. Even the notorious Babi Yar massacre—in which tens of thousands of the Jews of Kiev were marched to the ravines of Babi Yar, outside of the city, and there mowed down with machine guns by German soldiers—is presented in Soviet documents in a way which carefully eliminates any indication that the victims were Jews. To this day it is forbidden to erect on the mass graves in Babi Yar any Jewish monument to the memory of those executed. The same is true also in other Soviet cities and towns where the Jews were slaughtered en masse by the Nazis. The only known exception is in Vilna.

Since there are in the Soviet Union no Jewish history textbooks extant to record for the future generations on the martyrdom of Soviet Jewry during the Nazi holocaust, the Soviet authorities are gradually achieving their aim: to erase from memory the fact that Jews were the principal victims of the Nazi barbarities during the German occupation period.

The survival of Jewish life in the Soviet Union also depends to a very great extent on whether the Soviet Government will ever permit the formation of a central representative body of Soviet religious Jewry, as is permitted to all other religions in the country. So far, Jews have not been allowed to establish such a representative body.

The importance of the existence of such a central religious council, composed of representatives of the sixty remaining synagogues in the country—and recognized by the government as the spokesman for these synagogues—lies in several factors. Under the existing Soviet regulations only such a body can present the religious needs before the Soviet central authorities dealing with religious affairs. Without such a central council, each synagogue is isolated from the rest of the Jewish houses of worship in the country and is therefore exposed to the whims of local authorities without being able to complain to higher instances through its central body. It can thus easily be closed down by the local authorities without anybody knowing about it, not even the religious Jews in the nearest town.

The establishment of a central Jewish religious body embracing all the Jewish houses of worship in the country—such as that of all other religious groups in the Soviet Union—would also enable individual religious Jews in the hundreds of towns in which there no longer are functioning synagogues to seek guidance on ministering to their religious needs in circumstances where their communal religious life has practically been eradicated by the liquidation of their houses of worship. Contact with such individuals, who still number in the tens of thousands and who are determined to maintain their religious traditions under all circumstances, would contribute not a little to Jewish survival in many parts of the country where Jews are scattered, from the Baltic area to distant Siberia, from Moldavia to the Caucasus, and from Carpatho-Russia to the lands of Central Asia.

The establishment of a central religious council could also be of great importance to the survival of Soviet Jewry since it could serve as the address through which Jewish religious organizations in other countries could come to the aid of faithful Jews in the Soviet Union by providing them with ceremonial objects needed for the performance of religious services but unobtainable in the Soviet Union today. There is no such "Jewish address" today although other faiths have such official addresses and communicate freely with their coreligionists abroad on their religious problems.

No such communication is possible at present between Soviet religious Jewry and religious Jewish communities in other countries. Not even between the aged Moscow rabbi, Yehuda Leib Levin, and the community in Jerusalem, the oldest Jewish community in the world. This at a time when other religions in the Soviet Union continue their contact with Jerusalem, as the cradle of the world's major religions, even now, despite the severance by the Soviet Government of its diplomatic relations with the government of Israel.

Soviet Jewry—will it survive or disintegrate and disappear within a generation? The answer to this question lies in the hands of the rulers in the Kremlin. So far, there is no indication that the Soviet Government is inclined to encourage Judaism in the Soviet Union as it encourages other religions in their activities within the country and in their religious contacts with groups outside the country.

The remarkable thing is the fact that in all other Communist countries Jewish religious communities are permitted to have their central representative body, embracing the synagogues and other religious institutions. This is the case in Rumania, where the central Jewish religious body is even permitted to issue a trilingual publication—in Rumanian, Hebrew, and Yiddish—serving the religious interests of Rumanian Jewry. Moreover, Chief Rabbi Dr. Moses Rosen even represents Rumanian Jewry in the Bucharest parliament and is permitted to visit not only Israel but any Jewish community abroad. He has been to the United States several times and was permitted by the Rumanian Government to participate in international Jewish gatherings in Geneva in the interest of the Jews in Rumania.

The case is similar in Hungary, where Jewish religious communities and institutions are represented by a central body. There is even a Jewish Theological Seminary in Hungary, providing the communities with graduate Orthodox rabbis. The central Jewish body is allowed to maintain contact with Jewish religious groups abroad and is not hindered in its religious educational activities.

In Yugoslavia, the Jewish religious communities are banded into a federation recognized by the government. The Federation publishes a printed bulletin for Jews, keeping them informed on the communal activities. It also publishes a yearbook in the Yugoslav language, reflecting the Jewish cultural and communal activities for the year. No obstacles whatsoever are presented to leaders of the Federation about participating in international Jewish conferences abroad.

A central Jewish religious body also exists in Czechoslovakia, and even in Communist Poland, where government anti-Semitism has reached extremes and where Jewish cultural institutions have practically been liquidated since the anti-Jewish campaign started in 1967. A federation of the few synagogues that are scattered in about a dozen cities still exists, however. At one time, this Federation was permitted to publish a traditional Hebrew calendar giving all the data on Jewish religious holidays and carrying biographies of famous Orthodox spiritual leaders of various periods. This calendar no longer appears.

• • • 20

Will Moscow Permit Mass Emigration of Jews? Will Jews Emigrate If Permitted to Do So?

WILL THE SOVIET GOVERNMENT permit mass emigration of Jews from the country, as requested by Jews of the free world? . . . And will many of the three million Soviet Jews leave the U.S.S.R. if the doors for emigration open to them? . . .

I have tried to find the answers by speaking to government officials on the first question and to various elements of Soviet Jewry on the second.

Soviet officials, when reminded that their Premier, Alexei N. Kosygin, stated during a press conference in Paris—on December 3, 1966—that Soviet Jews who wished to join members of their families abroad were free to do so, claim that this is still the policy of the Soviet Government. When reminded that this does not seem to be the case, judging from protests by Soviet Jews to the United Nations about their having been refused exit visas to join their relatives in Israel, the officials try to evade the issue by asserting that since Moscow does not maintain diplomatic relations with Israel at present, emigration of Soviet Jews to Israel is being looked upon as an expression of taking the side of Israel in the Soviet-Israel rift.

When the fact that some of the Jewish applicants for emigration visas have been arrested, or dismissed from their jobs, is brought to their attention, the officials deny it; but when they are presented with names and verified cases in which the affected Jews addressed themselves with written complaints to top Soviet leaders in the Kremlin, the officials argue that the measures were taken not because of the applications for emigration, but because the applicants allegedly indulged in "Zionist propaganda," which has been prohibited in the Soviet Union since the early years of the Communist regime.

One of the Soviet officials with whom I had the opportunity to discuss—in 1968—the possibilities for Jews to leave the Soviet Union, realizing that his answers to my questions did not impress me, indulged in lifting somewhat the curtain hanging over the question of Jewish emigration from the country.

"I can tell you," he said, "that despite the fact that we consider the State of Israel an enemy, and notwithstanding the fact that we broke diplomatic relations with Israel in 1967, our authorities are still granting exit visas today to Jews who had applied for emigration to Israel before 1967. It is true that the number of such visas is small, but the very fact that we are still issuing them should serve as proof to you that we are not arresting Jews who apply for emigration."

He thought for a while, as if deciding whether he should go further, and then continued: "You may believe me or not, but what I am going to tell you now is exactly what happened with regard to Jewish emigration from our country to Israel. In the years before we broke off relations with the Israeli Government, there was a considerable number of Jews, mostly elderly, who applied for emigration visas. The majority of them were residents of the Baltic territories and of cities like Czernovitz, Kishinev, and others which became part of the U.S.S.R during World War II.

"As you know—and this is no state secret—our machine does not act fast when it comes to considering applications for emigration. So when we severed diplomatic relations with Israel in the summer of 1967 there were many applications for emigration visas upon which no decision had yet been made. Probably fearing that it might be held against them if they remained on record as seeking emigration to Israel now that Israel is considered a hostile country, a very large proportion of the applicants rushed into the local OVIR—the Soviet police division which deals with screening people for exit visas—and requested the return of their applications, emphasizing that they are no longer interested in joining their relatives in Israel.

"What did we, in Moscow, do about this situation? Strange as it may seem to you and to others in the United States, we sent instructions to the local OVIR offices to discourage the obviously frightened applicants from withdrawing their applications. The OVIR officers were told to explain to the applicants that they need not fear that their applications for emigration to Israel would be held against them. The officers were instructed to tell the applicants that in view of the severance of diplomatic relations with Israel there might be temporary inaction on their applications, but that action on them would be resumed at the first opportunity.

"I do not know whether the applicants, when told this, believed it to be the truth. However, among those who did not withdraw their applications at that time there are some who recently received their emigration visas. We have begun to take action on the pending applications and are slowly summoning applicants in various cities to grant them the visas they sought, provided their documents are in order.

"At first some of these applicants were surprised when they were summoned and informed that the exit visas were ready for them. But now no one is surprised when called to get the visa requested several years ago. In fact, if you go to Israel today you will probably find hundreds of Soviet Jews there who obtained their visas recently after a long wait during which they probably gave up hope of ever getting positive action on their applications."

"Does this mean that the gates of the Soviet Union will be wide open for Jewish emigration if and when the Soviet Government resumes diplomatic relations with Israel?" I wanted to know.

"That is a question which I am in no position to answer at this time," the official replied. "All I can tell you is that our government intends to stand by the statement made by Premier Kosygin on permitting Soviet citizens to emigrate if they wish to be reunited with members of their families abroad. Incidentally, we have been permitting emigration not only to Israel but also to the United States, Britain, Australia, and other countries when the applicants have proven that they are to be reunited with their relatives. The number of applicants for emigration to these countries is, however, very insignificant."

Studying the question of the possibility of Jewish emigration from the Soviet Union on the spot, one must come to the basic conclusion that there is no free emigration for Soviet citizens, although officially the Soviet Union ratified the United Nations Declaration on Human Rights, which states in Article 13, paragraph 2, that "everyone has the right to leave any country, including his own, and to return to his country."

On January 22, 1969, the Soviet Union also ratified the International Convention on Elimination of All Forms of Racial Discrimination, wherein the same idea on emigration is expressed as in the Declaration on Human Rights. This made Jews in the Soviet Union who have relatives in Israel bolder in their demand for exit visas for the purpose of being united with their relatives in the Jewish state.

Since then, Soviet Jews have felt more daring than ever before in seeking from the Soviet authorities permits to join their close family members in Israel, even though the Soviet Government openly and actively participates in the Arab war against Israel. The strong anti-Israel propaganda conducted almost daily in the Soviet press and over the Soviet radio does not deter Jews in the Soviet Union from applying for permits to emigrate to Israel. In so doing they feel that their request is backed by Soviet law and by international agreements signed by the Soviet Government.

So strong is their feeling in this respect that quite a number of them have, individually and collectively, addressed petitions to the United Nations, seeking the intervention of this international body when they have been refused Soviet exit visas. Today one can find many such petitions in the headquarters of the United Nations—some handwritten, some typed—filed away on the thirty-first floor. Once they are received, they never see the light again.

During recent years, the United Nations has been receiving thousands of letters each year complaining about the treatment of Jews in the Soviet Union and about other violations of human rights. All that is being done with these letters is that each complainant who gave his name and address is sent an official notice stating that the United Nations, as an intergovernmental organization, does not deal with communications from individuals or groups. Some of the Soviet Jews therefore try to submit their petitions for emigration to the United Nations by also sending copies to the Israeli Government, as was the case with a group of eighteen Jewish families in Soviet Georgia in August 1969, and with another group of twenty-five Moscow Jewish residents who at about the same time expressed their desire to leave the Soviet Union for Israel.

In both cases, the petitioners signed their names and gave their residential addresses in the Soviet Union. The petition of the Moscow Jews was addressed to U.N. Secretary General U Thant and to the President of the Twenty-fourth Session of the U.N. General Assembly in 1969. But it was suppressed by Mr. U Thant and was not even distributed among the members of the General Assembly, despite the request to this effect by the Israeli delegation at the United Nations.

Some Jews in the Soviet Union, obviously aware of the fact that their appeals to the United Nations will never see the light, addressed their requests for emigration visas directly to Premier Kosygin, or to Leonid Brezhnev, Secretary of the Communist Party in the U.S.S.R. When getting no action, the applicants manage to reach foreign correspondents stationed in Moscow with copies of their petitions. Such was the case in 1969 with a group of thirty-nine Jews in Moscow, with twenty-one Jews in Leningrad, with twenty-five Jews in Riga. The

Soviet authorities feel very embarrassed when these appeals appear in the foreign press, especially the American press. They react by making other Jews sign letters opposing Jewish emigration to Israel, as was the case with a letter signed by 102 Jews in Kiev and published in *Izvestia*.

In quite a number of cases Jews were arrested when they insisted on their right of emigration to Israel. Such was the case with Boris Kochubiyevski, a thirty-three-year-old Jewish engineer whose petition for emigration resulted in his being sentenced in May 1969 in Kiev to three years in a prison camp. In Riga in April 1969 a Jewish student, Ilya Rops, set himself on fire in a public square in protest against being refused an exit visa to Israel.

On the other hand, the Soviet authorities permitted the emigration to Israel of Nechama Lifshitz, the very popular Jewish folksinger whom Moscow has always cited as proof that there is no suppression of Jewish concerts in the Soviet Union. Applying for a visa to emigrate to Israel at a time when she was a tremendous success as a singer of Jewish songs and was appearing all over the Soviet Union was a very daring act on her part. It was a challenge to the Soviet regime, a way of emphasizing that despite her success she did not feel at home in the Soviet Union and did not want to be used as propaganda that Jewish culture is not being suppressed in the Soviet Union when it actually is being suppressed.

In her case, the Soviet authorities could not afford to arrest her or to make a case against her, news of which would have reached public opinion abroad, where her name was very well known. She was therefore granted permission to leave for Israel in accordance with the international obligations signed by the Soviet Government and ratified by the Supreme Soviet of the U.S.S.R., that "every citizen has the right to leave any country, including his own."

The determination of some Jews to leave the Soviet Union found its expression at the end of 1969 in a plot by a small group to hijack a Soviet twelve-passenger plane. The plot failed and two of eleven defendants were sentenced to death. The sentence aroused world-wide protests and the two death sentences were commuted and changed to long terms of hard labor. For three other prisoners sentences were also reduced.

Determination to emigrate to Israel was also displayed by a number of sit-ins staged by large groups of Jews—one group numbering more than one hundred people—in the reception room of the Supreme Soviet building. These daring demonstrations, as well as the increasing number of letters addressed by individuals and groups of Soviet Jews to top leaders in the Kremlin, resulted in the issuance of 470 exit visas to Jews during the first three months of 1971 as compared with about 1,000 issued during all of 1970. In 1969 the number of Jews permitted to leave the Soviet Union for Israel reached about 3,000. In the first four months of 1971 about 2,500 Jews received emigration visas.

Soviet authorities in Moscow estimate that 13,000 exit visas have been issued to Jews in the last ten years. But they ridicule reports abroad that 300,000 visas may be issued in the next few years. Figures on the number of Jews permitted during the last years to leave the Soviet Union are treated as confidential and have never been made public.

To make Jewish emigration more difficult, the Soviet authorities have at the end of 1970 raised the price of a passport tenfold, from 40 to 400 rubles. In addition, Jews, if they receive permission to emigrate, must also pay another 500 rubles as special tax for renouncing Soviet citizenship. This would make the equivalent of about $1,000 in U.S. currency at the official rate. The average monthly income of a person in the Soviet Union is about 150 rubles, thus a Jewish recipient of a Soviet exit visa has practically to pay the equivalent of six months wages for himself and for each visa granted to members of his family. University graduates have to pay an additional 500 rubles and a high school graduate 300. This innovation, will naturally affect negatively the possibility for many Jewish families to emigrate.

In Moscow I was told in 1968 by Jews that it is estimated that more than seventy-five thousand Jews in various parts of the U.S.S.R. have applied for emigration to Israel. This is indicative of the resolve of thousands of Jews to leave the Soviet Union for Israel. Many would also leave for the United States, Canada, and other countries to join their relatives there.

You speak to some of the Jews in Moscow, Leningrad, or Kiev who dared to defy the Soviet hostile attitude toward Israel and to apply to the authorities for emigration to Israel— without knowing what consequences such an application might bring—and you get a picture of the mood of the Jewish population. The elderly applicants still live with the fear of the latter years of the Stalin regime, when anti-Semitism reached a peak similar to that of the Czar's time and, in some instances, was even worse. They want to leave the country in order to be among Jews. Many of them want to live the rest of their lives in Israel for religious and sentimental reasons.

Among the younger people who risk seeking emigration to Israel despite the Kremlin's outspoken anti-Israel policy, the feeling prevails that for them the time for fear has passed as long as they can refer to the Soviet Constitution. They assert that under the Constitution they have a right to emigrate. Their mood of defiance is in many respects similar to the defiance shown by those young Russian intellectuals who seek self-assertion in literature, on the stage, and in freedom of expression.

Strange as this may sound, it is the violent Soviet propaganda against Israel that prompts many of the younger Jews to think favorably of Israel. These young Jews are far from being nationalistic. They have no Jewish traditions in their homes, they know no Jewish history, the Jewish languages are alien to them; they are assimilated and would never have known that they are Jews had this fact not been indicated in their identity documents.

The shrieking anti-Israel propaganda which the Soviet propaganda machine has developed since 1967 is only helping the curious young Soviet Jew to find out that somewhere there are brave Jews in a country of their own fighting for their independence and courageously resisting not only Arab attempts to destroy their country but also Soviet attempts to do so. This courage appeals to his imagination. It opens new avenues of thought in his mind. Like many Russians who don't believe what they read in their own press, he too takes the anti-Israel reports in the Soviet newspapers with a grain of salt. He sees them in a different light than that in which they are presented; he reads between the lines. And he is stimulated to look for an opportunity to emigrate to this brave little country which he knows is free and democratic.

It would be exaggerating to say that this is the case with the majority of the Jewish young people, but I came across a good number of those who speak openly of their desire to go to Israel. One of them, who applied for an emigration visa, told me:

"To you my request for an exit visa to Israel may seem daring, but to me it is not. It is not against the existing Soviet law to apply for an emigration visa. My applying for it does not mean that I am anti-Soviet but just that as a Jew—so described in my identity document—I want to live among Jews. There is nothing anti-Soviet in that. I consider that I may have an objective chance of securing the requested emigration permit and I took this chance. So do others if they have relatives in Israel."

Another young Moscow Jew who applied for an emigration visa found it difficult to explain to me why he, or other young Jews like him, should feel such a strong desire to go to Israel, since he had no Jewish education and knows nothing about Jewishness. He stressed that he does not feel that life in the Soviet Union is so bad for him as to force him to seek an opportunity to leave the country. In fact, he even went as far as stating that he does not know whether life would be easier for him in Israel, which is, after all, a country at war. He found it necessary to add that he personally had not experienced any anti-Semitism.

"Yet my heart is in Israel," he said smilingly. "I am all prepared to go there. I only hope that I will get an exit visa. If refused, I will try again and again. You can now go as high as sending a complaint to Premier Kosygin, who pledged that such visas will be issued to people having relatives in Israel."

Reference to Kosygin's pledge can be heard again and again

in talks with Jews in various cities in the Soviet Union, since the Premier's statement, made at a press conference in Paris, was also published in the Soviet press. It is this statement, too, that stimulated many Jews to dream about applying for permission to leave for Israel and to actually apply for it upon receiving the necessary invitation from relatives in Israel.

The fact that the Soviet authorities, although actually at war with Israel, have now begun to permit a trickle of emigration to Israel by Jews who long ago applied for reunification with their families there would seem to indicate that if the Arab-Israeli war—in which the Kremlin is so involved—were to end, the Soviet authorities might consider permitting large-scale emigration to Israel.

There is no free emigration today from the Soviet Union. The Soviet press never mentions the word "emigration." The country is hermetically closed for Soviet citizens wishing to leave it. Nevertheless, a large-scale emigration of Greeks who were Soviet citizens and who insisted on moving to Greece was permitted. Most of these Greeks had been residing in Russia since the time of the Czar and many of them were even born in the Soviet Union. They were allowed to depart for Greece by way of the Odessa harbor in large groups, without any mention being made in the Soviet press of this mass emigration.

In a similar case, large transports of Poles were permitted to return to Poland following World War II. During the war years—when they escaped from Nazi-occupied Poland to the Soviet Union—many of them married Soviet citizens and now have children who were born in the Soviet Union. Yet after the war they were given permission to return with their families to Poland if they wished to do so. No difficulties were made about their Soviet-born spouses and children leaving the country with them.

People from the Baltic countries which became part of the Soviet Union after World War II—Lithuanians and Latvians—are now permitted as individuals to emigrate in very limited numbers to the United States for reunification with their families. Nothing is mentioned about it in the Soviet press, since emigration from the Soviet Union is generally banned. It would be easy for the Soviet Government to explain to its non-Jewish population any large-scale Jewish emigration to Israel if the government were to decide on a policy of permitting such large-scale emigration.

By permitting large-scale emigration of Jews the Soviet Government could reduce the number of Jews in the country, doing it at the same time as an act of compliance with its international obligations to enable reunification of families broken since World War I. The Soviet press would hardly report any mass emigration of Jews from the country, just as it did not report the mass emigration of Greeks. Some non-Jews in the Soviet Union would probably be envious of the fact that Jews were being permitted to leave the country, but the majority of the non-Jewish population would hardly consider it a special privilege for Jews. They would be more likely to look upon it as a move on the part of the government to reduce the number of Jews in the country, and many would even welcome it.

But will Jews in the Soviet Union engage in large-scale emigration if it is permitted?

Most of the Jews who hitherto applied for emigration to Israel are those who live in the territories acquired by the Soviet Union after the war—Lithuania, Latvia, Galicia, Bukovina, and former parts of Rumania. These territories came under Soviet rule many years after the Soviet regime was established in Moscow. Their inhabitants still remember their traditional Jewish life under non-Soviet government, with Jewish culture flourishing, Jewish religious observance unmolested, and the teaching of Hebrew unsuppressed. Today, under the Soviet regime, they miss this freedom and they make no secret of the fact that they consider Judaism a very important element in their life.

Similarly, there are the Jewish communities in the mountainous Caucasus region which are very religious and where the more than fifty years of Soviet rule have not wiped out the deep feelings for Jewish traditions and for the ancient Jewish

hope to see Israel reborn. Even under Stalin—and maybe because of Stalin's being a native of the Caucasus—they, like
the rest of the population, were never harassed by the Soviet
attack on religion to the extent that people in other parts of
the Soviet Union were. Their Jewish communal life and aspirations are still being shared today, even by the younger elements of Jews, those who were born under the Soviet regime
but who are Jewishly educated.

Then, too, there are many Jews in Soviet Ukraine who because of the undiminishing anti-Semitic feelings there—
strengthened by the Nazi propaganda during the years of the
German occupation and encouraged later by Khrushchev,
who was practically the ruler in Soviet Ukraine under Stalin
prior to his becoming the head of the Soviet Union—do not
feel much at home in their native land, where they suffer all
kinds of discrimination. They are not as religious as the Jews
in the Caucasus and are far from being as Jewishly concerned
as the Jews in territories acquired by the Soviet Union after
World War II. But they definitely feel they are second-class
citizens.

In all of these three segments of the Soviet Union a great
number of Jews look forward to the possibility of emigration
to Israel. This number would definitely increase if large-scale
emigration were permitted. However, the case may not be the
same with Jews in the Russian part of the Soviet Union, although there are Jews there today who also openly apply for
migration to Israel.

The Jews in the Russian Soviet Republic—which is the
largest in the Union of the Soviet Socialist Republics—are
very much assimilated, the majority of them having been born
or having grown up under the Soviet system. They have no
Jewish background. The Jewish religion means nothing to
them because they are not religious. But the existence of Israel
intrigues them, inasmuch as their identity documents stamp
them as being of Jewish nationality.

If large-scale emigration to Israel were permitted by the Soviet authorities quite a number of the Jews of that part of the
Soviet Union—where the majority of the Jews reside today

—would probably want to visit Israel, for which they have a warm feeling as a Jewish country. Whether they would like to proceed to Israel in order to settle there forever is a different question. There are among them a good many scientists, physicians, people active in the arts of the country. Many of them are thoroughly assimilated. Quite a large proportion of them are intermarried. Like many of the Russian intellectuals they are not happy about the lack of freedom in the country but they are, like all the Russians, adjusted to it. They are unhappy with the fact that their identity documents carry the word "Jew." But they live in the hope that the day will come when this "disability" will be corrected by the government.

Of the approximately three million Jews now residing in the Soviet Union, there would, in my opinion, still be more than two million left even if large-scale emigration from the Soviet Union to Israel and other countries is permitted. It must be assumed that any sizable emigration of Jews will have to be adjusted to the capacity of Israel to absorb them, since Israel's population is only about three million and especially since many of those permitted to emigrate would be elderly persons. It could take perhaps ten years to bring over five hundred thousand Jews from the Soviet Union to Israel should so many care to leave, and ten years is a long time during which all kind of developments might be possible in the Soviet Union.

As matters stand now, it is obvious that the Soviet Government will not permit any large-scale emigration of Jews to Israel while the Arab war with Israel goes on. Moscow is too much involved in this war. The Kremlin is strongly on the side of the Arabs and against Israel. But it would be wrong to think that the question of permitting Jews to leave the Soviet Union for Israel is a closed chapter.

High Soviet officials in Moscow, when you mention the subject of Jewish emigration, give you the impression that the subject is very much on the mind in the Kremlin but is being held in abeyance for the time being. When the Arab-Israeli war is over and relations between the Soviet Union and Israel are reestablished, the Soviet Government may not be averse to permitting Jewish emigration to Israel on the basis of family reunification even though emigration is otherwise banned. It is of course to be expected that if the Soviet Government would permit family reunification on a large scale, there will be Soviet Jews who will seek emigration also to the United States and Canada where they have their relatives. This aspect of Jewish emigration from the Soviet Union has however not found any vocal expression among Soviet Jews for the time being.

♦ ♦ ♦ 21

Good-Bye, Moscow

THE HUGE AUSTRIAN PLANE flying between Moscow and Vienna picks itself up from the earth on the Moscow airfield and rises higher and higher into the clear blue sky. The passengers—most of them foreigners, but some also Russians —have seemingly all flown before on Soviet planes inside the Soviet Union. They feel the comfort and relaxation which one does not feel when flying on a Soviet plane from Leningrad to Moscow, or from Moscow to Kiev, or from Kiev to Odessa, and other distances.

The Austrian stewardess, well-mannered and in an elegant uniform which one does not see on Soviet planes even on international flights, appears on the aisle between the rows of seats with an armful of newspapers ready to distribute among the passengers.

"What would you like to read?" she asks me in German, approaching my seat. "Shall it be the London *Times*, the Paris edition of the *Herald-Tribune*, *Le Monde*, Swiss newspapers, Austrian newspapers, West German newspapers? . . ."

Hungry for several weeks for any newspaper appearing in the free world, I ask for several of them in various languages. I get them with a charming smile. So do some of the other foreign passengers. The Russian passengers are careful. They ask for newspapers appearing in Communist countries. They get them.

"I could kiss you!" the passenger sitting next to me tells the stewardess when receiving from her the newspapers he wanted. "You brought me back to the civilized world! . . . Now I can catch up on what is going on in this world! . . ."

He speaks loudly and the passengers around him smile. They can understand his exuberance. They, too, feel as if they had restored contact with the wide world. No longer are they dependent on the Soviet press and radio which angle the presentation of news to suit Soviet propaganda interests.

The girl smiles pleasantly over my neighbor's elated remarks, but says nothing. She hears such remarks not for the first time. There are passengers on each flight from Moscow to Vienna making such remarks. True, the newspapers she distributes are a day or even two days old, but the news they contain is still new and fresh to anyone on the plane. Most of the news has not appeared in the Soviet press, and the world events which the Soviet newspapers did carry were presented not in their true perspective. Reading international news in Soviet newspapers is like looking into a crooked mirror.

During the weeks I spent in the Soviet Union I was completely isolated from world events. And so is every foreign visitor. I wanted to know about the developments in the United States, in Vietnam, in the Middle East, but I could hardly get a clear picture of what is actually going on from reading the Soviet press. This despite the fact that I learned to read the Soviet press between the lines, as some do. Every item I read was colored by obvious propaganda. The newspapers did not even pretend to show impartiality. The reports were full of adjectives showing plain bias.

For foreigners in the Soviet Union who read no Russian, there are Polish, Czech, Hungarian, and East German newspapers sold on the newsstands at every large hotel. But these newspapers are all Communist organs of the countries in which they are published. There is almost no difference between their contents and the contents of the Soviet press. In a way, they are provincial editions of the Moscow press, emulating the Moscow system of presentation of news and following the Moscow line of propaganda in their editorials and commentaries.

If you are an American citizen and you are interested in following up the world news as it really happens, you can go to the United States Embassy in Moscow and read brief news bulletins there giving the highlights of the news of the last twenty-four hours as received by the embassy. But entrance to the American Embassy is being watched very closely by Soviet police and secret service men. They stop you and demand to see your documents. And this is unpleasant and discouraging. I had to show my American passport to a Soviet uniformed policeman standing near the entrance to the embassy. He insisted on knowing whether I am really an American. Later, when I left the embassy building through a side door, I faced the same experience with a Soviet secret service man in mufti stopping me a few steps from the embassy premises and asking me to identify myself.

You read the Soviet newspapers one day and another and a third, and you get bored reading them without finding any true reflection of what is really going on in the wide world. The result is that on the fourth day you discontinue reading them. Then you are really isolated from contact with the outside world. You begin to understand how unavoidable it is for the Russians to become indoctrinated and to see the world through Soviet eyes.

Serious non-Communist Russians realize that their press tells them half-truths and that the news which the newspapers do present are Communist-colored. Some of them dare to listen to foreign radio stations which are beaming their Russian-language broadcasts from London and West Germany to the Soviet Union. But this is an illegal act, and one has to be very careful of his neighbors before he indulges in such an act.

With the Arab-Israeli situation being very tense—and the Soviet press and radio following the Kremlin line of being pro-Arab and violently anti-Israel—numerous Jews in the Soviet Union risk listening to their radios at a certain hour when broadcasts from Israel in the Russian language are di-

rected to Soviet listeners. This is their only real source of news
on what is happening on the Arab-Israeli front and what role
the Soviet Government plays in the Middle East developments.
They read in the Soviet press the anti-Israel version of the
news of the day and compare it with the broadcasts they hear
illegally from Israel, thus seeking to get a balanced picture.

The average Soviet citizen is, however, not very much interested in what is going on outside of his country. He is ignorant of world affairs. He leaves it to the government to do the
thinking for him as far as foreign affairs are concerned. He
does not like the Arabs, for instance, and cannot understand
why his government sends so many goods and military equipment to the Arabs when there is a shortage of goods in the
country for its own citizens. But this to him is high politics.
And he is indifferent to high politics.

The average Soviet citizen is interested only in one thing as
far as Soviet relations with the outside world go—in peace.
There is no family today in the Soviet Union which has not
been affected by the German-Russian war. Almost every family lost one or more members in this war. In addition many
thousands of homes were destroyed by the war.

The word "peace" is therefore a very meaningful word to
everyone in the Soviet Union, and the Kremlin is aware of it.

The great majority of the Soviet people are kept in complete
ignorance of how life is in the democratic world. When they
are told of some events, it is usually in a distorted form. The
Russians have, therefore, no understanding of the actual life in
countries like the United States, England, France. In effect,
they live as though on a different planet than the people of the
free world.

American and other foreign movies are seldom shown in the
Soviet Union. Soviet authorities are afraid to have them shown
because the Soviet people might become "infected" with some
aspects of "capitalistic life." The normal way of American life
shown in the movies is poison to the Soviet mind. The scenes
that show workers and average Americans having automobiles,
living in comfortable homes, enjoying better furniture and
modern kitchens, watching television, wearing stylish clothes,

constitute a denial of what the Soviet people read about the
United States in their press. The Soviet authorities prefer to
show pictures of slums in American cities and of poverty demonstrations.

As a result, the average Soviet man and woman do not understand many scenes in foreign films picturing American life.
To them the better ways of American life are completely
alien. It is like showing to Americans movies of life in the
distant lands of Asia and Africa. Life in these lands is so different in the eyes of Americans, and so is life of Americans different in the eyes of the average Soviet viewer of American
films, if and when he is permitted to see some of them.

A Soviet engineer, one of a group, who was sent by the Soviet Government to study the production methods of American automobile factories, frankly admitted to me that he was
bewildered by many things in the American way of life in the
first days of his stay in Michigan. He was impressed not only
with the comforts of the daily life of the average American as
compared with that of the average Russian, but also with the
democratic form of life which he had never experienced before.

"Among the things that impressed me most during the first
days of my work in one of the largest automobile factories,"
he confided to me, "was the fact that one cannot tell the difference there between an ordinary worker and a supervising
engineer. Both work in overalls, both eat in the same factory
cafeteria, but appear equally well dressed at the end of the
day's work when they get out from the overalls, both have automobiles in which they come to work and drive home from
the company's parking lot after work. There is no visible class
distinction between them as we have it in the Soviet Union
where the engineer is considered a superior being. . . .

He returned to the Soviet Union with a better understanding of the American way of life and with a different view of
the position of the average American worker. He still considers the United States a "capitalist country dominated by Wall
Street." On this he did not change his mind. He thinks the
state rather than Wall Street should get the profits between
the producer and the consumer. But he has learned to under-

stand things in American life which the great majority of the people in the Soviet Union—those who cannot even dream of being permitted to visit a democratic country—do not understand.

The average Russian does not understand, for instance, when he reads in his newspapers about the mass strikes of workers in American industrial enterprises. No strikes can ever take place in factories in the Soviet Union where labor unions are under complete control of the state. No Russian worker or employee would ever dare to speak about declaring a strike because this would be tantamount to calling for a revolution against the system. No Soviet union leader would tolerate it.

The average Russian does not understand also when he reads in his papers about street demonstrations in the United States. He is completely puzzled by the fact that they take place so freely. In the Soviet Union, hostile demonstrations take place only when they are inspired by the government against an outside "enemy" state. They disperse as soon as the police want them to disperse. To attack the police, as is the case in the United States, is unheard of in the Soviet Union. This would be tantamount to a revolution against the authorities.

It is similarly puzzling to the Russians when they read in their press about student disturbances in American universities. Such disturbances on campuses would be intolerable in the Soviet Union. Their leaders would be arrested and punished. The mildest punishment would be deportation to a remote place never again to reside in a university city. Incidentally, the Soviet press is very careful about reporting student disturbances in America or anywhere in the free world, lest Soviet students be infected with the idea of indulging in demonstrations.

To the Russians it is also strange that people in the United States carry placards with insulting inscriptions about the President of the nation and nothing happens to them. None in the Soviet Union would dream of appearing in the street with placards carrying slogans against the head of the state. He knows in advance what would happen to him. Another fact that the Russians are puzzled about is the abusing scenes in American courts. They cannot understand why they are being tolerated.

The Negro issue is also something they don't understand. Colored people, whether Americans or Africans, are not liked by the people of the Soviet Union in spite of the fact that the Soviet Government claims to be the defender of their causes. Few black people are seen in Moscow. In other cities one does not see them at all. Most of the colored people are students sent for indoctrination to Soviet schools. But they are kept practically isolated in their dormitories. One cannot see a black student with a Russian girl. There have been cases where Russian students have beaten up Africans seeking the attentions of white girl students.

The Negro issue in the United States is not fully comprehended not only because the dislike of the average Soviet man and woman for colored people—or for this matter also for people of the "yellow race"—but also because the Russians don't know of the term "equal rights" in the American sense. This term is alien to them. They therefore fail to understand why white people in the United States are pro-Negro and are demonstrating for Negro causes.

The Soviet press makes a lot of propaganda about the increase in crime in the streets of American cities. The average Soviet citizen does not understand why the American authorities cannot cope with this problem. It seems strange to him that the banks are held up, that people are robbed by teenagers in the streets and that nothing seems to stop them. The older generation of Russians remember the early years of the Bolshevik Revolution when homeless urchins who lost their parents in World War I or in the revolutionary battles roamed the streets of Moscow, Leningrad, Kiev, and other large cities. Hungry, dirty, and ragged, they attacked people in the streets in packs, like wild animals. They would surround their victims, biting them, stabbing them, tearing their clothing, and robbing them of watches and other valuables.

These terrorist activities by juvenile delinquents came to an end when the Soviet authorities began to round up the animal-like youngsters. They surrounded them in the streets, they raided the railway stations where many of them made their homes, looked for them in hallways of dilapidated buildings where they usually slept, hunted them at the bazaars, and sent them to special camps where they were isolated and kept under strict discipline. While in detention they were given psychological treatment, and education.

In a short time the wild urchins disappeared from the streets and with them also the problem of street crime. Of the many thousands of "bezprizorny"—homeless and wild urchins—the majority were sent to military units after being "restored" to normal behavior and were absorbed by the armed forces. Quite a number of them later held command positions in the Red Army and excelled in battle during World War II.

The average Soviet citizen, who actually looks up to the United States, is confused. He fails to understand why in a country like the United States drastic measures against crimes are not introduced as in the Soviet Union. He also cannot understand the growing problem of drug addiction among American youth. The problem is alien to him, because he knows of no drug users in the Soviet Union.

Nor can he figure out why pornographic literature and films are permitted in the United States, even glorified in some cases as freedom of human expression. Not that the average Russian is a Puritan—far from it. But he considers pornography in print and in film to be in bad taste and a factor which demoralizes the youth.

All this lack of understanding of certain factors in American life is due to the fact that the people in the Soviet Union, being isolated from the rest of the world, have acquired a different mentality than that of the free world. They see everything through Soviet glasses. To them, the government is not the servant of the nation but the ruler over the nation. They have accepted the Czarist dictatorial system for three hundred years, and it is therefore psychologically easier for them to accept the present dictatorial system of Communist rule under which they have already been living for more than fifty years.

Just as the American way of life is little understood by the Russians, so is the Soviet way of life alien to most Americans visiting Russia.

American visitors in the Soviet Union, when they discuss

problems of Soviet life with educated non-Communist Russians who are aware of the defects of the Communist system, find it puzzling that these people—among them men and women who bitterly criticize the Soviet restrictions on freedom of expression—are at the same time loyal citizens of their country. Most of the critics believe that the Soviet system is better for the Russian people than the "capitalist" system, except for the muzzling of free thinking.

The average Soviet citizen does not think in intellectual terms. He also does not dream of having a look at life outside of his country. He is nonpolitical. His interest is centered only on things that affect his immediate daily life. These are primarily food, clothing, housing, education of his children, health care for himself and his family, old age pension, and similar necessities.

He feels less exposed to the fear of the possibility of his being arrested than do many of the men holding high positions. During the Stalin regime no high official—whether military or civilian—was certain that he might not be arrested tomorrow for one or another reason. This was the case even with high officers of the dreaded political secret service. No commandant of a slave labor camp in Siberia, or elsewhere, was ever certain that tomorrow he might not be a prisoner in the camp which he administers today. So was also the case with generals, factory directors, and people high in the Communist Party hierarchy. The higher the post one held, the lower he stood to fall.

Not so with the small man. The gray citizen was deeply concerned over the arrests of his neighbors and the "disappearance" of his factory director. But he himself felt he had nothing to fear, if he only continued to keep his mouth shut. And this he has been doing for many years anyway. The political trends within the country were not uppermost in his mind, and to events abroad he paid no attention at all. He took the regime as it stood.

With regard to the United States, the average Soviet citizen maintains a position that no anti-American propaganda on the part of his government and press can change. He admires anything that is produced in the United States—from an automobile to a razor blade. He does not believe that "capitalist America" is interested in starting a war against his country. He was not told by his government the truth of the extent of aid given by the United States to the Soviet Union during the war with Germany, but he knows that such aid was given in large quantities of food and in military equipment. He also looks up to England and France as civilized countries, although he knows practically nothing about them. He hates Germany because he cannot forget the destruction the Germans brought on the Soviet people during the war and the invasion years.

He knows that he is destined to live the rest of his life in no other land than the Soviet Union, and is loyal to his country. Although he often feels the difficulties of daily life under the Soviet system, he also appreciates the benefits. He is submissive and has no special ambitions except to exist.

He is satisfied with the fact that the state takes care of his children from nursery age, all the way through public school, up to and including a university when the youngster deserves higher education. He is satisfied with the care taken of his health by the medical system which is free. He likes to think of the fact that he will be receiving a pension after he reaches a certain age and at the same time also be permitted to work for regular wages, if he chooses to do so. All these factors did not exist under the Czarist regime. He does not know that they exist in other countries, in some even on a more generous scale.

The average Soviet citizen may be dissatisfied with the fact that he must live in a crowded dwelling and share the kitchen and the toilet with other occupants on the same floor. He is grumbling that he has no privacy for himself and his family. However, he looks forward submissively and hopefully toward the time when he will be assigned a two-room family apartment, with a kitchen of his own, in some of the new apartment buildings which are being built, mostly in the large cities, in an attempt to solve the housing problem. Practically every resident in Moscow, and in other large cities, is on a registration

list, awaiting his turn for an apartment. And rent is unbeliev-
ably low in the Soviet Union, whether in an old or new apartment.

The average Soviet citizen may also be dissatisfied with the
fact that there is a shortage in some goods—primarily clothing and shoes, which are very expensive and of a low quality
—but he appreciates the fact that he no longer has to stand in
line for bread, meat, and other foodstuff, as was the case for
many years. He sees slow improvement in his daily life since
World War II and takes it for granted that things will improve even more if the country will only not be involved in
another war.

This is why the word "peace" is very meaningful to him.
He is perhaps proud of the fact that his country is next to the
United States in developing atom bombs and in sending vehi-
cles to the moon, but the possibility of an atomic war frightens
him. He is not afraid that the United States will start such a
war, but he reads the news about China and considers China a
greater danger to his country than the United States.

The average Jew in the Soviet Union sees things practically
the same way as the average Russian, except that he has the
feeling that he is treated as a second-class citizen. He may be
proud of the fact that Israel is proving itself a country of great
courage and creative ability, but in essence he remains a loyal
Soviet citizen. He has proven this in the war years with Germany by the proportion of decorations received by Jewish
servicemen for bravery on the battlefields, and he has proven it
also in peacetime by his contributions to the development of
Soviet science, technology, and culture.

In the face of the present policy of the Kremlin to discriminate against Jews in certain fields of life, and to look upon
them with a certain amount of distrust, it is strange to learn
that Jews in the Soviet Union are considered by other national
minorities there as a pro-Russian element and as "russifiers."
This is held against them by nationalist Ukrainians and in the
Soviet Republics in Central Asia which are jealously guarding
their own national language and culture. It is being cited that
in the census of 1959—more than ten years ago—76.4 per-

cent of the Jewish population declared the Russian language as their mother tongue, whereas 75 percent of the German population in the Soviet Union declared German as their national language not to speak of other national minorities. No other national group in the Soviet Union declared Russian as its native language to the extent declared by the Jews.

About 20 percent of the Jewish population declared Yiddish as their native language. But most of these were from territories acquired by the Soviet Union after World War II—the Baltic countries, Eastern Poland, Bessarabia, Bukovina, and Ruthenia. In most of these territories the Russian language was hardly known by the Jews who had been living a full cultural and religious life of their own before the Stalin-Hitler pact in 1939. The Jews in Soviet Bukhara, Dagestan, and Georgia have their own national culture, speak no Russian, and know no Yiddish.

Although many Jews would welcome permission to emigrate to Israel—as many non-Jews would welcome permission to emigrate anywhere—the great majority of the Jewish population feels that their destiny is in the Soviet Union. They see a picture of two million Jews—two-thirds of all the Jews in the Soviet Union—remaining in the country even after twenty years of intensified emigration. They are aware of the fact that Israel is absorbing about sixty thousand newcomers a year from the whole world. At this rate it would take a generation to bring out a million Jews from the Soviet Union even if the Soviet Government would permit mass emigration of Jews to Israel. And a million Jews is only one-third of the Jewish population. Not to speak of the fact that during the twenty years of intensified emigration there will also be new births among the Jews in the country, with the birthrate probably exceeding the death rate.

The large majority of the younger and more assimilated Jews in the Soviet Union therefore think not in terms of emigration but rather in terms of securing equality of opportunity and of Jewish cultural regeneration. They would like, for instance, to see the Soviet authorities permitting the publication of Jewish history textbooks at least in the Russian language.

They know nothing of Jewish history, since the subject has not been taught in the Soviet Union even in the years when Yiddish schools were still existing before the liquidation by Stalin of all Jewish cultural institutions.

Like most of the people in the Soviet Union, the Jewish people are part of the "great silent majority" in the country. They accept the existing Communist regime as the millions of other people do. The largest part of them, having been born and raised under the Soviet regime, live—like the rest of the population—in an isolated Communist world. Their life is so different than the life of the Jews in the free world.

They are the nationality treated worst in the Soviet Union. Yet, because of their creative minds, they constitute a great asset to the development of the country in the fields of science, technology, industry, medicine, and general culture. This, despite the obstacles they face because of the special government policy with regard to Jews. They would certainly be of even greater service if the obstacles were removed.

World Reaction to the Soviet Policy on Jews

HOW DOES THE FREE WORLD react with regard to the Soviet treatment of its Jewish population? How do prominent non-Jews react? Has there been any reaction in Washington and in other capitals of democratic countries? Has the United Nations reacted?

Many prominent personalities throughout the world came out with public statements denouncing the Soviet policy on Jews. They include the eminent British philosopher Bertrand Russell, usually known for his sympathy toward the Soviet Union; Dr. Martin Luther King, Jr.; Dr. Albert Schweitzer, the great humanitarian; Queen Elizabeth of Belgium; U.S. Supreme Court Justice William O. Douglas; Bishop James A. Pike; leading American labor figures like George Meany and Walter Reuther, and hundreds of scholars, authors, scientists, and men prominent in public life. They all called on the Soviet Government to restore to Soviet Jewry the rights and institutions to which Soviet law entitles them.

A public address delivered by Dr. King on Soviet Jewry in 1966 in New York on a nationwide hookup has provoked a feeling of discomfort among Soviet leaders who claim to be the defenders of the black people. So did the protest by Lord Russell. So disturbed was the Kremlin by Russell's call for justice to Soviet Jewry that Nikita Khrushchev, as Soviet Premier, found it necessary to answer him. Dr. King's 1966 address on the treatment of the Jews in the Soviet Union was rebroadcast in 1968 at a mass meeting of American Jews at which the death of the great leader of the black people was mourned.

More than thirteen hundred faculty members of some one hundred U.S. colleges and universities issued, in 1970, a "Declaration on Solidarity with Soviet Jews." They expressed shock "at the campaign of vilification, intimidation and coercion conducted by the Soviet regime against its Jewish citizens." The text of the declaration, carrying the signatures, was made public in leading American newspapers and copies of it were sent to Soviet Premier Alexei N. Kosygin and to Leonid L. Brezhnev, head of the Communist Party in the Soviet Union. Over three thousand faculty members of more than one hundred and fifty universities and colleges also addressed an appeal to the Twenty-Fourth Congress of the Soviet Communist Party, in 1971, to permit large-scale emigration of Soviet Jews seeking reunion with their families abroad, and to restore Jewish cultural and communal rights.

Similarly, more than two thousand Protestant and Catholic clergymen in the United States issued under their signatures "A Letter of Conscience" urging the Soviet Government to abate its repressive measures against its Jewish citizens. Such collective appeals to the Soviet Government were also addressed—and made public—by leading American actors and writers. Attention to the Soviet policy of discrimination against Jews was similarly focused at special meetings of intellectuals in London, Paris, and other capitals of the democratic world.

The Council of Europe in Strasbourg, France, which is the organization of European states, took an interest in the treatment of the Jews in the Soviet Union and circulated the results of its study made on this subject. The International Commission of Jurists in Geneva made a similar study. The

Socialist International in London conducted two studies. The findings in all these studies were critical of the Soviet Union.

The Soviet policy on Jews was criticized even within the ranks of the Communist Party in the United States, Canada, England, France, Italy, and the Scandinavian countries. Maurice Thorez, the late chief of the Communist Party in France, had sent a leading member of the party, Chaim Sloves, to Moscow to investigate the situation on the spot. Sloves returned to France with a report which touched off considerable internal debate within the leadership.

A delegation of the Communist Party in Canada was also sent to Moscow. It included J. B. Salzberg, a Jewish leader of the party. After talks in Moscow on the Jewish question with Premier Khrushchev and other men of the Kremlin, Salzberg returned to Canada and resigned from the party.

In 1960 a Conference on Problems of Soviet Jewry was held in Paris. The participants were intellectuals from various countries known for their friendly attitude toward the Soviet Union. The statement adopted at this conference said that the participants have gathered "to discuss dispassionately and without partisanship the situation of the Jewish minority in the Soviet Union." After analyzing the status of Soviet Jewry, the statement appealed to the Soviet Government "to examine the position of the Jewish minority and grant it the opportunity for full national and cultural self-expression, as enjoyed by other Soviet nationalities and guaranteed by the Soviet Constitution."

Similar was the request voiced at a two-day conference of distinguished personalities in Latin American countries held in 1970 in San Jose, Costa Rica. The parley was attended by leading men in the political, social, and cultural life of eleven Latin American countries and was devoted to "the study of the situation of the Jewish minority in the Soviet Union." It had the official support of the Costa Rican Government and was attended by three Cabinet members despite the fact that the government was at that time negotiating a commercial agreement with the Soviet Union, for the sale of coffee. The agreement was signed while the conference took place.

President Jose Figueres of Costa Rica sent a message to the conference expressing "solidarity" with its aim, and emphasizing his "affection for the Jews (in the Soviet Union) who are now facing anguishing moments." The conference, which was conducted under the chairmanship of Professor Carlos Monge Alfaro, rector of the University of Costa Rica, appealed for the rights of Soviet Jewry and urged the Organization of American States (OEA) "to interest their respective governments to consider the problem of Soviet Jewry, and to instruct their representatives at the United Nations to discuss this problem at the meetings of the General Assembly and at the Commission on Human Rights of the United Nations." The conference also decided to promote the creation of national committees in Latin American countries to be of help to Soviet Jewry, as well as the creation of a permanent International Committee —composed of representatives of Latin American countries, the United States and European countries—for the same purpose.

In the United Nations the Soviet policy on Jews came up for discussion every year during the last few years, with the Soviet Union being charged with violating the Universal Declaration on Human Rights. More than fifteen governments have raised the problem of Soviet discrimination against its Jews in speeches at the General Assembly, the U.N. Economic and Social Council and the U.N. Commission on Human Rights. Among them are the United States, Israel, Canada, Great Britain, and France, but included are also Italy, Denmark, Australia, New Zealand, Uruguay, and a number of underdeveloped countries like Dahomey, Sierre Leone, Madagascar, and others.

The view of the U.S. Government has especially been brought out sharply by Mrs. Rita E. Hauser and Ambassador Morris B. Abram, members of the U.S. delegation to the United Nations. Speaking at sessions of the Human Rights Commission, each of these two U.S. representatives were firm in their criticism of the Soviet restrictions of human rights with regard to Jews. Mrs. Hauser especially aroused the ire of the Soviet and Ukrainian delegates at a session of the Third Committee of the General Assembly in November 1969, when she cited the harassment of Soviet Jews by reading a letter from a Jewish mother in Moscow addressed to the U.N. General Assembly. The Soviet and Ukrainian delegates interrupted her several times at the session when she read the letter.

Mr. Abram was attacked bitterly by his Soviet counterpart at the Human Rights Commission, Yakub Ostrovski, for drawing attention to Soviet treatment of Jews at a meeting of the Commission. The Soviet diplomat went as far as to point out in a derogatory manner that Mr. Abram was a Jew. This was in itself considered an anti-Semitic act since never before has any speaker in the United Nations referred to the religion of any of the delegates there. The malicious outburst of the Soviet delegate evoked a formal protest to the Soviet Mission to the United Nations by Secretary of State Dean Rusk.

The United States is second only to Israel in seeking to bring about a change in the Soviet policy with regard to the Jews in the Soviet Union within the framework of human rights. However, the State Department emphasized, in a position paper on the Jews in the Soviet Union in 1967, that it has found from experience that its government-to-government approaches to Soviet officials on all levels were "totally ineffective."

Israel is, of course, in front at the United Nations in bringing up the situation of the Jews in the Soviet Union at every possible occasion. Verbal duels between representatives of Israel and the Soviet Union on the status of Soviet Jewry have become a permanent part of the discussions on human rights at the United Nations. The Soviet diplomats continue to brush aside the accusations that Jews are being deliberately discriminated against in their country by the government. They claim that there is no "Jewish problem" existing in the Soviet Union.

Nevertheless, the Soviet Government expressed opposition to the idea of appointing a United Nations High Commissioner for Human Rights. It even indicated that it would boycott him, if appointed. The naming of such a High Commissioner—similar to the existing post of U.N. High Commissioner on Refugees—was first urged in 1963 by

Jacob Blaustein who had served as a member of the U.S. Delegation to the United Nations. It is now under discussion by U.N. organs. The establishment of the post of a High Commissioner on Human Rights would make it possible for the United Nations to conduct inquiries on violations of human rights not only in the Soviet Union but also in other countries. It would enable the U.N. to receive petitions on infringement of human rights and to study them. It could be instrumental in helping to find constructive solutions to problems arising out of infraction of human rights.

Numerous governments and many of the nongovernmental organizations accredited to the United Nations and concerned with human rights strongly favor the establishment of a post of High Commissioner for Human Rights. The great majority of the more than two hundred nongovernmental groups—national and international—which enjoy consultative status in the United Nations feel deeply against racial and religious discrimination. They are sympathetic with the efforts to alleviate the situation of Soviet Jewry.

Representatives of the Soviet Union find themselves often in conflict with representatives of nongovernment organizations at meetings of United Nations bodies when discussing human rights. They must defend themselves whenever the question of the treatment of Jews in their country emerges there. Soviet delegates therefore mounted, in 1969, a virtual assault against the accredited organizations specializing in human rights programs, particularly Jewish ones.

Nine international Jewish organizations have been granted accreditation on a consultative basis by the U.N. Economic and Social Council which deals with human rights problems. Soviet representatives on the Council—joined by Arab representatives—challenged the nongovernmental status of the World Jewish Congress, the Coordinating Board of Jewish Organizations, and other Jewish international groups enjoying accreditation. They singled out the B'nai B'rith for special attacks. As a result, the United Nations undertook a review of its system of accrediting nongovernmental groups. This system was incorporated in the U.N. Charter which provides for a consultative's relationship between the U.N. Social and Economic Council and nongovernmental organizations.

The sentiments in Washington with regard to the Soviet treatment of Jews can be projected from the fact that ninety U.S. Senators and 357 members of the House are on record as having appealed to the Soviet Government to restore to the Jews in the Soviet Union their full cultural, religious, and human rights. Also from the fact that every President of the United States—from Truman to Nixon—has publicly displayed deep interest in the fate of Soviet Jewry.

President Dwight D. Eisenhower had expressed his concern about the status of the Jews in the Soviet Union to Soviet Premier Nikita Khrushchev when the two met at Camp David on September 25, 1959, during the latter's visit to the United States. President John F. Kennedy made no secret of his feelings about the discriminations against Jews in the Soviet Union. President Lyndon B. Johnson, in a lengthy public statement, emphasized that "the position of the Jewish community in the Soviet Union is a matter of deep and continuing concern to me, to this Administration, and to millions of thoughtful people throughout the United States."

Pointing out that the United States cannot ignore the existence of religious or racial persecution anywhere in the world, President Johnson declared: "In the Soviet Union today there is grave governmental, social, and economic pressure against Jewish culture and religious identity." He cited the "harassment of synagogues" and the "interference with the training in the great cultural heritage of Judaism which has given the Jewish community such vigor and endurance through many centuries."

He revealed that "all responsible officials in the U.S. Government continue to search for practical methods of alleviating the position of Soviet Jews" and that he instructed the U.S. representative to the United Nations Human Rights Commission to propose an article on anti-Semitism in the draft convention on the elimination of all forms of racial discrimination. Over the vigorous objections of the Soviet delegate, an article was adopted by the Commission reading: "States-parties condemn anti-Semitism and shall take action as appropriate for its speedy eradication in the territories subject to their jurisdiction."

But when the draft convention containing this proposal was presented later for a vote to the Third Committee of the U.N. General Assembly, the Soviet delegation made a counterproposal suggesting that states-parties condemn not only anti-Semitism but also Zionism, Nazism, all forms of colonialism, hatred, and inhumanity. By deliberately equating anti-Semitism with Zionism the Soviet delegation achieved what it wanted—the Committee passed a resolution eliminating all specification of racial hatred, thus, in effect, killing the U.S. proposal. The unmistakable reason for the Soviet maneuver was the apprehension that incorporation of such an article into the Convention would provide a permanent world platform for the airing of Soviet policy toward the Jews.

President Nixon, in a letter addressed to the American Jewish Conference on Soviet Jewry, expressed hope that "humanitarians throughout the world will continue vigorously to protest the restrictions and deprivations of human rights" under which the Jews live in the Soviet Union. Emphasizing that he deplores the Soviet policy of oppression, President Nixon pointed out that "Jews in the Soviet Union, even more than other religious and minority groups, are subjected to special disabilities." He added that he was "deeply concerned by the resurgence of the Soviet anti-Jewish campaign, thinly disguised as anti-Zionism—a campaign which is mirrored in Communist countries in Eastern Europe."

Secretary of State William P. Rogers, in a statement presented on October 1970 to more than five hundred students who met at the State Department—after two days of demonstrations to protest the treatment of the Jews in the Soviet Union—said that the Nixon Administration would do everything possible to improve the prospects for Soviet Jews to emigrate wherever they wanted to go.

"We have expressed sympathy and support on many occasions for persons in the Soviet Union who wish to emigrate, often to rejoin their families elsewhere, but who are denied permission to do so. We shall continue to make these views known and to take every practical measure which could help to overcome the hardships suffered by such persons," Secretary Rogers pledged. A similar statement was made by British Foreign Secretary Sir Alec Douglas-Home in November 1970.

Of special interest was an address delivered on behalf of the U.S. Government on September 19, 1965, at a session of the U.N. Economic and Social Council by Ambassador James Roosevelt. Speaking at a session on the problem of Soviet Jewry, and emphasizing that "this problem must concern the United Nations," Ambassador Roosevelt drew a comparison between the situation of the Negroes in the United States and that of the Jews in the Soviet Union. He pointed out three "profound" differences:

> 1. Our American society, beginning with the President of the United States, recognizes that the problem of Negro rights is our great moral problem, with all its additional political, economic and psychological ramifications. But, in the Soviet Union, the authorities have consistently refused to recognize unequivocally that a grave problem of anti-Semitism exists there.
>
> 2. American Negroes have a growing opportunity to take their fate into their own hands, and they are doing just that through the great and inspiring civil rights movement. But Soviet Jews are utterly helpless and voiceless, and any attempt on their part to combat discrimination and to advance their group rights would be immediately suspected and shattered by official action.
>
> 3. Our public opinion and our public institutions are moving to support the goals and aspirations of the Negro Revolution. But in the Soviet Union, a large segment of popular sentiment is itself anti-Semitic, and that segment which opposes anti-Semitism can at best speak in muffled and obscure tones. As for Soviet public institutions, the hard fact of the matter is that it is government policy which is the guilty party.

Top Negro leaders expressed similar sentiments. Dr. Martin Luther King, Jr. said in a letter to *The New York Times* (January 10, 1965) that he was "profoundly shocked by the treatment of the Jewish people in the Soviet Union." Declaring that he wanted to add his voice "to the list of distinguished Americans of all faiths who have called the injustices perpetrated against the Jewish community in the Soviet Union to the attention of the world," Dr. King stated: "The struggle of the Negro people for freedom is inextricably interwoven with the universal struggle of all peoples to be free from discrimination and oppression. The Jewish people must be given their full rights as Soviet citizens as guaranteed by the Constitution of the U.S.S.R. itself. The religious and cultural freedom of this old Jewish community should be re-established. In the name of humanity, I urge the Soviet Government end all the discriminatory measures against its Jewish community. I will not remain silent in the face of injustice."

Bayard Rustin, prominent civil rights leader, echoed Dr. King's views. "Injustice to any people," he said, "is a threat to justice for all people. That is why—as a Negro living in the United States—I will not be silent, or fail to be concerned about what happens to my brothers and sisters who happen to be Jews in the U.S.S.R. What happens to them happens to all of us here—and we must be concerned. So our demand is that the Jewish people must be given their full rights as Soviet citizens and as human beings." James Farmer, another prominent Negro leader, expressed his "concern and outrage at the denial of equal religious and national rights to Jews in the Soviet Union."

As chairman of a public tribunal in New York arranged by the Conference on the Status of Soviet Jews—a national organization sponsored by prominent Jews and non-Jews—Mr. Rustin submitted an eleven-page report of the findings of the tribunal to the Soviet Embassy in Washington. Dr. King was one of the sponsors of the Conference on the Status of Soviet Jews. Its executive secretary is Moshe Decter, an expert on Soviet affairs.

The American Jewish community, with its population of close to six million, is naturally in the forefront of the fight to secure the restoration of full rights to Jews in the Soviet

Union. As the "older brother" living in a country where it can raise its voice of protest freely on behalf of Soviet Jewry, the American Jewish community watches very closely developments with regard to Jews in the Soviet Union and reacts on them publicly and forcefully.

Participating in focusing attention on the situation of the Jews in the Soviet Union are all elements of American Jewry —rich, poor, and middle class; industrialists and workers; big business people and small traders; scientists, rabbis, physicians, lawyers; women's groups, and student organizations.

Leading in the program of exposure to public notice of the anti-Jewish practices of the Soviet Government is the American Jewish Conference on Soviet Jewry, a coordinating agency of twenty-six major national American Jewish organizations. Constituent members of this central body include the American Jewish Committee, American Jewish Congress, Jewish Labor Committee, Jewish War Veterans of the U.S.A., the central rabbinical organizations of all denominations in Judaism, B'nai B'rith, the Conference of Presidents of Major American Jewish Organizations, the National Jewish Community Relations Advisory Council—itself a coordinator of the work of Jewish national groups and local communities in the field of community relations in the United States—National Council of Jewish Women, Hadassah, Student Struggle for Soviet Jewry, North American Jewish Youth Council, and other important Jewish groups.

The staff headquarters of the American Jewish Conference on Soviet Jewry are located in the offices of the National Jewish Community Relations Advisory Council in New York, which provides it with professional guidance. The American Jewish Committee, which is affiliated with the Conference as one of the constituent organizations, plays a major role in servicing media and nongovernmental organizations with background material on the problem of Soviet Jewry.

The American Jewish Conference on Soviet Jewry, being the spearhead since 1964 of activities among American Jews on behalf of the Jews in the Soviet Union, is constantly increasing its activities in all directions. In 1968 it presented a thirty-two-page "White Paper on Soviet Jewry" to President Johnson at the White House. The same year, on Human Rights Day, the Conference submitted to the United Nations a petition with 250,000 signatures protesting the violation of Soviet Jewry's human rights. Under its auspices, peaceful mass demonstrations protesting Soviet treatment of Jews have been taking place in all the larger cities in the United States with tens of thousands participating in them. The Conference has also developed a sustained program of bringing the problems of Soviet Jewry to the non-Jewish population. Its leaders meet from time to time with U.S. government officials presenting, in private discussions, new facts on anti-Jewish developments in the Soviet Union.

Under the auspices of the Conference and of the Student Struggle for Soviet Jewry demonstrations of Jewish youth in solidarity with Soviet Jewry have been taking place in front of the United Nations building, Soviet Mission to the United Nations, and Soviet Embassy in Washington. The largest outpouring of Jewish youth took place in October 1970 in numerous communities including New York, Philadelphia, Los Angeles, Detroit, Miami, Cincinnati, Hartford, and other cities. In New York, more than fifteen thousand participated in such a demonstration. A two-day mobilization for Soviet Jewry organized by the North American Jewish Youth Council, the coordinating body of some twenty-five affiliated national Jewish youth groups with a total of seven hundred thousand members, attracted more than three thousand Jewish students from various cities to Washington where they held a peaceful hour-long march chanting slogans for full rights for Soviet Jews.

The organizations affiliated with the American Jewish Conference on Soviet Jewry, while endorsing such demonstrations, are sharply opposing the tactics of the Jewish Defense League —a small militant group—in its picketing Soviet cultural undertakings in the United States, like concerts of internationally known Soviet pianists and violinists. The American Jewish Conference is opposed to any violence and considers the tactics of the Jewish Defense League as being counterproductive.

In their peaceful demonstrations and activities the groups affiliated with the Conference call upon the Soviet Government for action on five specific demands:

1. To permit Jews throughout the U.S.S.R. freely to develop Jewish communal and religious life and institutions and to associate and work with comparable Jewish communities and religious groups inside and outside the Soviet Union.

2. To make available the educational institutions, schools, teachers, textbooks, and scholarly materials necessary to teach Soviet Jews the heritage, the languages, the history, the beliefs, the practices, and the aspirations of the Jewish people.

3. To permit its Jewish citizens freely to practice, enhance, and perpetuate their culture and religion by the establishment of appropriate institutions including places of worship, and other religious facilities, theaters, publishing houses, newspapers, and journals, and to remove all discriminatory measures designed to restrict this freedom.

4. To use all means at its disposal to eradicate anti-Semitism and discrimination against individual Jews and to require as the first step in this program the immediate cessation of the virulent anti-Semitic propaganda that has suffused the Soviet mass media since the Six Day War between the Arabs and Israel in 1967.

5. To permit Soviet Jewish families, many of whom were separated as a result of the Nazi holocaust, to be reunited with their brethren abroad and to implement the Kosygin promise of family reunion.

These demands were advanced to the Soviet Government also in a "Declaration of Soviet Jewry" adopted on February 25, 1971, at the final session of a three-day World Conference of Jewish Communities on Soviet Jewry held in Brussels, with seven hundred and fifty Jewish leaders from twenty-seven countries participating. Speakers at this conference included Arthur J. Goldberg, former U.S. Supreme Court Justice, and David Ben-Gurion, former Prime Minister of Israel.

The Conference pledged itself "to ensure that the plight of Soviet Jewry is kept before the conscience of the world until the justice of their cause prevails." The delegates declared solidarity with the Jews in the Soviet Union "in their heroic struggle for the safeguarding of their national identity and for their natural and inalienable right to return to their historic homeland, the land of Israel." The Declaration issued at the close of the Conference expressed concern for "the fate and the future" of the Jews in the Soviet Union. "We denounce the policy pursued by the Government of the Soviet Union of suppressing the historic Jewish cultural and religious heritage," it stated.

Is the Soviet Government sensitive to these mass protests by Jews and non-Jews and by the expressed dissatisfaction in the ranks of the Communist parties in democratic countries? Does a possibility exist that the Kremlin might reevaluate its policy toward Soviet Jewry under the pressure of world opinion?

There are indications showing that the Soviet Government is embarrassed by the fact that its image as "protector" of underprivileged nationalities is very much marred by the strongly negative worldwide reports of its treatment of the Jews in the Soviet Union. There is also an opinion prevailing that some elements in the Kremlin are unhappy about the Soviet policy toward the Jews.

When Anastas I. Mikoyan visited the U.S. in 1959 as First Deputy Premier of the Soviet Union, he met with the leaders of the prestigious American Jewish Committee. It was the first time that a top Soviet government leader consented to come to a luncheon arranged by a Jewish organization to discuss the treatment of the Jews in his country. The luncheon was a closed affair held at the Carlyle Hotel in New York, with Soviet Ambassador Mikhail Menshikov also attending. The two Soviet representatives were agreeable to a point where they even posed for a photo with some of the Jewish leaders to "immortalize" the meeting. The photo appeared in *The New York Times* showing Mikoyan, Menshikov, and Senator Herbert H. Lehman, Irving Engel, and Jacob Blaustein—the top leaders of the American Jewish Committee—all smiling happily.

At this intimate gathering, Mikoyan assured the Jewish

leaders that there was no fear that the Jews in the Soviet Union would be forcibly transferred to Biro-Bidjan, in Siberia, and physically segregated there. He denied reports to this effect. But at the same time, he insisted that the Jews in his country do not suffer religious, cultural, educational, and economic discriminations. Ten days later he was presented by the American Jewish Committee with a memorandum outlining the discriminations in detail. The memorandum was based on a report of the British Communist Party which launched a special investigation on the Jewish charges by sending an official delegation to Moscow, headed by J. R. Campbell, editor of the London *Daily Worker*.

The delegation's report, which later appeared in *World News*, the official organ of the British Communist Party, stated that the delegation "encountered many difficulties" in its investigation in Moscow. The report then went on to enumerate the discriminations the delegation found. The report not only confirmed the charges of Jewish organizations abroad, but it also brought out new facts. One of them was that the Soviet Encyclopedia, which in its 1932 edition devoted about 160 columns to Jews, reduced this in the 1952 edition to four columns, and that biographies of many prominent Jews had been removed. The conclusion of the Communist Party delegation, as expressed in the report, was that "many Soviet intellectuals must themselves be puzzled and confused, and indeed ashamed" of the Soviet policy on Jews.

In presenting its memorandum to Mikoyan, the American Jewish Committee, quoting at great length from the report of the British Communist Party delegation's findings, expressed hope that Mikoyan, as one of the top leaders of the Soviet Government, will take an interest in bringing about satisfactory solutions to the problems concerning Jewish life in the Soviet Union. However, nothing further has been heard from Mikoyan. The Soviet policy remained as outlined a year earlier by Soviet Premier Nikita Khrushchev to a visiting delegation of French Socialists. "Should the Jews want to occupy the foremost positions in our Republics now," Khrushchev told the Frenchmen, "it would, naturally, be taken amiss by the indigenous inhabitants. The latter would ill-receive their pretension." Khrushchev refused to see Jewish leaders when he visited the United States after Mikoyan.

Khrushchev's statement, as well as a statement made in Moscow by Mrs. Furtzeva, one of the leading personalities of the Soviet regime, who "explained" that Jews have been eliminated from positions because the government found "a heavy concentration of Jewish people" in some of its departments, reflect the dominating mood prevailing in the Kremlin even today. Soviet spokesmen, when confronted with questions on the treatment of Soviet Jewry, indicate practically that Jews are regarded as "outsiders."

With all this, the Soviet Government seems nevertheless to be worried over the growing waves of protests abroad against its relegating its Jewish population to a status of second-class citizenship by refusing to grant them the same rights enjoyed by all other nationalities in the Soviet Union. There was a time when the Kremlin ignored these protests. Later it began to argue that the treatment of its Jews is "an internal affair." Now one can read Soviet apologetic articles abroad—but only abroad—presenting a picture which aims to show that there is no discrimination against Jews in the Soviet Union. Little by little the Kremlin's official line on Jews bends under pressure from the civilized world. How long it will take to bring the Kremlin back to its original policy of the early years of the Revolution, when the accent was laid on equality for Jews with all other national minorities in the country, no one can tell.

INDEX